Swimming
Home

Praise for *Swimming Home*

'Judy Cotton activates sense memory with astonishing precision. Her descriptions of her early years in Broken Hill and Oberon and of her time in Sydney have a thrilling, almost cinematic concision. Cotton is brilliant on the dynamics of sibling and mother–daughter relations, and she gives the subjects of loss and longing an orchestral subtlety and richness. I read this book in awe – of Cotton's skill, yes, but also of the depth of her feeling for Australia.' —**Sebastian Smee, author and Pulitzer Prize– winning art critic for** *The Washington Post*

'Reading this wholly original memoir about home and family, about not belonging and rebellion, is like viewing a great exhibition. You move from one remarkable image to the next, back and forth through time, from one room to another, inhaling at the beauty before you, exhaling at the shock of some of it, always moving forward to a sense of peace, grace and understanding.' —**Caro Llewellyn, author of** *Diving into Glass*

'Judy Cotton paints like she writes and writes like she paints: fiercely, vividly and unpredictably … She's fearless when it comes to putting her mark on paper, or on screen. She is, however, also the incongruously well-mannered and dutiful daughter, and they exist in tandem with the wild girl of the high country … Judy is a puckish combination of indomitable heart, incisive brain, evil humour and eyes that see at 1/1000th of a second. And she renders that seeing into images with deceptive ease.' —**Diana Simmonds, journalist**

'*Swimming Home* is not only a powerful personal chronicle, but for those of us outside of Australia it provides a vivid sense of the heartbreak and triumph that has shaped that country.' —**Lowery Stokes Sims, US art historian and curator**

Swimming Home

Judy Cotton

Published by Black Inc.,
an imprint of Schwartz Books Pty Ltd
22–24 Northumberland Street
Collingwood VIC 3066, Australia
enquiries@blackincbooks.com
www.blackincbooks.com

9781760643539 (paperback)
9781743822388 (ebook)

 A catalogue record for this
book is available from the
National Library of Australia

Cover design, text design and typesetting by Akiko Chan
Cover artwork: *Dive* by Judy Cotton

Epigraph is from John Burnham Schwartz, 'A Stranger in Kobe', review of *The
Dream of Water: A Memoir* by Kyoko Mori, The New York Times Book Review,
5 February 1995.

The Dreaming story about Gurangatch and Mirrangan on page 51 is from the
Jenolan Caves website: www.jenolancaves.org.au/about/aboriginal-culture/
dreamtime-story-of-gurrangatch-mirrigan

Song on page 164 is 'Oh, Look At Me!' from the musical *Salad Days*,
lyrics by Dorothy Reynolds and Julian Slade, 1954. Reproduced by permission
of Alan Brodie Representation Ltd.

Every effort has been made to trace copyright holders and obtain their
permission for the use of copyright material. The publisher apologises for
any errors or omissions and would be grateful if notified of any corrections
that should be incorporated in future reprints or editions of this book.

For Yale Kneeland

'For a writer, exile from the land of one's childhood can sometimes prove the most certain way home. Especially when self-imposed, such distance yields a complicated equation of loss and gain. Lost, of course, is the tactile immediacy of the past, the physical evidence of experience. Gained is the costly freedom to remember, to turn place and time over and over in the imagination, all the while knowing that no one story can explain the past.'

John Burnham Schwartz, 'A Stranger in Kobe',
The New York Times Book Review

TRANSIT

Undertow is perilous, the Pacific riptide hauling me back hand over hand like a movie on rewind as I watch from the plane. Landing, I struggle to take off instead, but no matter how many times I leave, the land has me by the ankles with a grasp that won't let go.

This stolen continent hums like an ancient undetonated bomb counting down; its memories come like a thief in the night. The coast road abruptly transmits a vast sweep of cobalt ocean, while cicadas tick in gum trees overhead. Bird sound here is orchestral, echo and aria. '*Gong-gong, gong-gong,*' currawongs yodel, weaving sooty heads outside the window at dawn. Magpies wheedle with double-tongued cadence. Parrots squeak past in a jolting flirt of scarlet and green; cockatoos flare sulphur crests, ticked off for no reason. Harboured high in a Moreton Bay fig so huge its roots have a hundred-year lock on the shore, fruit bats chirk and shit.

I suspect the frangipani; that every giddy inhalation of their fragrance will spin me to sleep. I suspect the little luff of surf, beach rocks sculpted by time, shallow sea pools, the silky abrasion of sand. Be very wary. You will never leave here alive.

I

1923

Eve hid under the fig tree, articulating piano keys drawn in the silky dust – *C-D-E-F-G-A-B*-C – reverse – span the octave. Her right hand played treble. Repeat. A sea of dry red dust flowed under the cloak of shadowy fig leaves where she sat, spitting purple grape pips, her metronome for timing scales. Her dog, Mickey, snuffled after chittering hens. At night, Eve's fingers morphed into chicken beaks that pecked at red roses and bunches of violets on her flowered bedspread. In her dreams the beaks lapped with yellow feathers turned into snake scales, hard eyes in their tilting heads. Her sister's eyes were like that. Peck, peck, Eve practised her scales, one hand to peck, the other playing scales. Repeat.

She heard her sister undress, the rayon slip slither to the floor, the elastic snap of panties, an airy rustle of cotton nightgown settling over hair tied in curling rags. In the morning her sister, her beautiful sister Jean – everyone said so – would untie the rags, and auburn curls would spill to her shoulders. Under the bedspread Eve hummed to herself, building bridges and trestles from five-finger scales, grand structures of gem-studded gold that spanned the rivers of the world. Above them rolled vast cloudy skies where dragons wrapped themselves in chicken feathers and princes rode elephants among giant flowers.

As Archie lurched into the kitchen, Ollie pulled Eve and Jean from their beds to hide behind hydrangea bushes by the front verandah. She had planted copper pennies under them to turn the flowers blue. She was a good gardener, even though all she had to work with was the desert and harsh green water from the sluggish Darling River; laundry, kitchen and bath water saved for the garden. Rainwater from the tank stand was for drinking. 'If you wash your hair in rainwater and rinse it with vinegar, it brings out red highlights,' Jean whispered to Eve. They sneaked rainwater to rinse their hair.

When Archie slumped with a guttural snore to the waxed parlour floor, the girls tiptoed past their comatose father. Ollie's house was always clean despite her drunken husband, or else to spite him. Mickey curled up under Eve's bed and pulling the covers over her head, she heard a rustle of paper and found a bar of chocolate under her pillow. Archie beat her mother and Jean, but not her – not Bebe, the youngest. Holding chocolate wrapped in gold paper in one hand, she played scales with the other. She slept.

*   *   *   *

When Jean grew breasts, there was no avoiding the small volcanic cones that sprouted under her blue angora sweater. Below the fig tree Eve peered at her own chest under a cotton singlet but no effort of imagination fastened breasts onto her pale silky skin. She pushed her bare toes into the dust, placed two green figs in her singlet, and held it tight to see how she would look. She played scales in the dust, wearing her fig breasts.

It was my mother, Eve, who hid under the fig tree, under the grapevine, under the eiderdown, the tablecloth, the verandah. Years later she hid under caftans and cut her face from family photographs. But in my memory, it is her face I see clearest, laughing up at someone. Afterwards, she insisted she hadn't meant the laughter, that she had been working at 'making things go well'.

'Jean was the beautiful one,' she said. 'It was Jean everyone looked at.' Concealed under the verandah, Eve watched Jean slither past hungry male eyes and wondered why no one stared at her, at Eve. When at last they did stare, she turned her head away. I studied her as she weighed her life's balance against Jean's in a calculation of who had won, who had lost. By every count, Jean lost and Eve won. But Eve's victory felt hollow to her; all eyes had been on Jean when it mattered most.

Eve rated my sister and me by the same terms, and we both lost in the equation. She scored us on looks, clothes and marriages, having decided that achievement in the world was best left to my father. She worked hard to even things up between my sister and me, tying me down by one metaphorical leg so that I could not run faster than my blue-eyed older sister.

*   *   *   *

After three children, Eve's breasts grew larger than she had imagined under the fig tree. Six months before the start of World War II, the blue-eyed first was born. By now Eve was permanently estranged from beautiful Jean of easy virtue, who trailed a long line of broken love affairs in her wake like old shoes tied to a wedding car. If Eve had a love affair, she kept it to herself and married the man she met in the desert town of Broken Hill when she was two and he was four. At her birthday party she threw red jelly at him, branding him hers for life. He saw her again when she was seventeen and nudged his friend Dan. 'Ask her if she'll go to the pictures with me,' said Bob. 'Ask her yourself,' Dan replied. Bob asked, and from then on, they were united against the world – against her mother, her father, her sister, even against us, the three children of their union.

1927

As the summer heatwave reached 137 degrees in Broken Hill, Eve's fever rose. She fidgeted at tiny nosegays of violets, roses, oxeye daisies and cornflowers printed on her bedspread as they began to grow and take on lives of their own. She could smell the gaudy aroma of white and lavender sweet peas and gathered up petals as fragile as gauze to hold under her nose. But her hands were empty. Bunches of pink roses, thin, pliant freesia stems knotted around each other, levitated, and floated away with an aromatic snap. More flowers flew by, carnations, bachelor's buttons, Sturt's peas. The Sturt's peas raised their black and scarlet beaks and crowed. The hen roosting on Eve's chest slowly folded coal-dark wings over her face and stole her air.

A sandstorm sieved fine red grit through every pore of her mother's polished house, prying into the linen closet, fingering dresses and coats, shrouding shoes, cups, and plates, wringing out the oxygen. Red powdered Eve's pillow, cloaking her eyelashes and hair. As the sky turned black with dust, car headlights shone green. There was no way to tell where Ollie's polished floor met the rug. It was Eve's job to wipe off jars and tins in the pantry after a storm. Lying feverish in bed, she heard tins and cups smash onto the floor.

Sitting beside Eve's bed, Ollie dredged a cloth through a bowl of water, swinging it back and forth to cool it before sponging her daughter's burning face. There was no ice, no fan, only plaintive wind, clogged air and ceaseless heat. Eyes closed tight against the sand, Mickey howled. He was not allowed into the room where Eve tossed and muttered, bouquets of flowers evaporating in her hands. Beside their house on William Street, a camel train passed on its way into the desert. The Afghani driver wound a cloth over his nose and mouth and, lowering his head against the prevailing grit, headed deep into the Australian outback. Dust blurred all definition as the camels blew green snot from large soft nostrils and stumbled past the barricaded houses at the edge of town, before turning north into the bewildering confines of the trackless centre. Scarlet Sturt's peas were crushed beneath their wide splayed feet, mirages that haunted the desert sky dissolved, and flocks of kangaroos and emus were erased in the blank inland sea of red dust.

*　　　*　　　*　　　*

Years later, Eve would tell us about 'the Ghan train' coming from the east end of town, stalking slowly past where she sat, blank and listless, on the small verandah of the house, watching it pass as if it were simply a fevered image from her illness. Outside the stone wall, a huge mound of sand had piled after the dust storm. Her neck still encased in plaster, Eve was home at last from hospital, where she had been confined, sweating with fever, for six weeks, head held upright in a flannel-lined wooden box, neck wrapped in gauze and plaster. The hospital had smelt of Dettol, stale dishwashing water and old tea. It was hot, and her neck was itchy. Somewhere, someone cried. The nurses in stiff caps and white pinafore aprons were tired: 'Don't whine, Eve. Think of the starving children in India.' Eve wheedled instead – 'Can I?' 'Will you please?' – earning the nickname 'Bebe the Wheedler'. The walls of the hospital were green, the iron bedsteads painted cream, striped ticking mattresses stuffed with horsehair. The nurses smoothed the sheets and tucked the corners so tightly that Eve came to love the feel of flat, unwrinkled sheets. She slid her legs on them. Overhead, a fan turned aimlessly, as heat mounted through the long afternoons. On the taut green bedspread Eve practised *Moonlight Sonata*, her boxed head propped against a starched pillowcase.

After six weeks, Eve was allowed to walk down the hall of the hospital to the lavatory, carefully holding her boxed head upright. 'Don't sit on the seat!' Ollie told her. 'Think of the germs.' Later, Eve would say to us, 'My poor mother. She caught buses and trams to bring me food in hospital.' There was no ice, no ice cream to bring from a town milk bar, the way my cousin Tony brought me ice cream years later when my tonsils were removed in the small country hospital of Oberon. Tony was our best friend, a year younger than me, son of my father's eldest sister. He sat crimson with embarrassment, ice cream melting in the green glass dish, because the matron had put me in the maternity ward with women who had just given birth. The new mothers tried to incite me to wet the bed to annoy the nurses, who seldom answered bells rung for help.

'Why did you stop playing the piano?' I asked Eve years later, knowing that pleading with her to play again would not change anything, and that the Steinway with dragon-shaped silver candle holders on each side would sit silent, except for the occasional party. 'Because I would never have been as good as I should have been,' she replied. What did that cost her? Little Eve, Bebe the Wheedler, Bebe, the baby, the role she played with masterly precision, pianissimo and fortissimo.

'Never wash me with Palmolive soap. It sickens me,' Eve said to me. 'They washed me with it in hospital.' Smelling of Palmolive soap and rigidly collared in plaster to prevent her neck twisting, Eve was sent home. But her neck vertebrae were now slightly awry, and the illness so sapped her strength that her body was always two paces behind her iron determination. She had Scheuermann's disease, a condition in which the spine grows unevenly and the vertebrae become wedge-shaped. It left her with a small permanent hump and an itch. Ollie scratched under the cast with a long knitting needle. As children we scratched Eve's back with a long bamboo wand that had tiny, curled fingers carved at one end.

Eve was acutely sensitive to noises and smells, to the look of things, her ears like bee antennae homing in on the pollen of sound. She had migraines so acute she would lie motionless for three days in a darkened room. I would creep in and examine her nostrils to see if she was still breathing – her body was so inert she seemed dead. It turned out that her migraines were genetic, and I would inherit them. Eve's internal organs and vertebrae were slightly compressed from the disease, and she had constant back pain. As children, we called it 'Herback' because we thought she was faking it.

Eve's hypersensitive musical ear seemed able to translate the language of bees, mice, frogs, cicadas, chickens and ducks, sheep, dogs, cows, foxes, plants, trees and birds into her secret personal score, the song of the earth itself. She could trace the merest fraying of tone, and anything slightly off-key irritated her skin, her very bones. At sixteen Eve won first prize for senior pianoforte at the Convent School of Music on Mica Street, in November 1934. A well-known critic described her performance as 'a pleasurable surprise'. Her prize was a long string of crystals, which she gave to me after I helped steer her through her first heart bypass. They seemed an apt metaphor for her adamantine self: a length greater than expected, crystalline, complicated, hiding their beauty inside a velvet box, difficult to wear. I gave the crystals to my eldest niece, the one with a voice like a musical instrument, after she sang Eve's passage to death with the aria 'Thou, All My Bliss'. Eve died to music exactly at noon on 27 July 2000. She liked to be on time.

*   *   *   *

At fourteen, Eve was sent to her aunt in Neutral Bay to study piano at the conservatorium. It was 1931, and she rode the train alone from Broken Hill, seven hundred miles west of Sydney, passing miles of Sturt's peas, flocks of kangaroos and emus, watching mirages of water light up the sky. The names of passing stations were as familiar as a musical score: Wilcannia, Cobar, Nyngan,

Narromine, Menindee, Ivanhoe, Condobolin, Parkes, Dubbo, Wellington, Orange, Blayney, Bathurst, Tarana, Rydal, Lithgow, Katoomba, Penrith, Blacktown, Parramatta, Strathfield. She had changed trains at Bourke to the steam train that trundled through mallee scrub and groaned up over the Blue Mountains until the green of the east coast came into view. There, Eve saw the ocean she grew to love so much she never wanted to lose sight of water again. Her aunt owned a big house in Neutral Bay on Hayes Street. Eve slept there outside on an upstairs verandah. 'You couldn't do that now,' she said, when she showed me the house sixty years later. The house was called 'Kcot-Cedar', her aunt's surname, Radestock, ravelled for its label. 'We used to catch the tram to Balmoral to swim,' Eve said. My sister's house of long silences overlooks that beach now. On the corner of Eve's aunt's house, a huge old frangipani is blooming.

'Was it there then?' I ask, but Eve doesn't remember. I try to buy her a frangipani to plant in the small garden of her apartment, but no, she doesn't want one – this woman – who rode the train from Broken Hill alone at fourteen and saw the Sydney Harbour Bridge made whole at last, the two halves having met in the middle the year before – is very particular about what she wants. The most particular person I have ever met.

1931

Isidore Goodman, a tall, thin man from Cape Town, was Eve's pianoforte teacher at the conservatorium in Sydney's Botanic Garden. Eve was serious, consistent, precise, and her precision pleased him, perfectly poised fingers ranging the keys expertly, wrists held level, body erect, pedal used only as noted in the score. She sat firm and steady as she played, obedient to the concept that swaying with the melody was melodramatic and disrespectful to the composer. Her ideal was Bach. By twenty she was ready for public performance, but when the choice came between that or marriage, she opted for the latter, wearing a long white satin dress, and carrying a bouquet of waterlilies. The pressure from her husband's desire to rise in the world, and the birth of three children during World War II, eventually cancelled all her piano dreams. She focused instead on perfection, orchestrating a Bach-like sonata and fugue of domesticity, setting impossible standards achieved at her own peril. Ours too.

*   *   *   *

Jean was a beauty in a small desert town. Jean was 'fast', the first in the family to divorce, a real scandal at that time. But in the old days of Broken Hill, she was just a spirited beauty who wanted more than she could ever have. While Eve sweated out her illness, harnessed in plaster, Jean grew breasts, small plums that ripened into melon globes that could shake a room. Never one to waste time, Jean flashed her sparkling eyes, trying them out on the local youths. Jean had 'it', and young men lay in wait, hoping to bump into her accidentally at the chemist or the bank. 'Where are you going Jean?' 'Want to go to the pictures?'

Jean shed the pleated skirts, lace collars and angora sweaters that Ollie favoured for tight crepe dresses cut on the bias, outlining every curve. The 'picture show' morphed into fast times at the West Darling Races, cigarettes, men in fancy roadsters, picnics, balls oiled with too much liquor and limbs loosened under the stars at Silverton, everything and everyone going too fast. Soon, Jean married an older man, despite the fact that he was Catholic; her big perfect teeth gleamed under a sharply tilted hat, her two-piece suit of tightly tailored sky-blue crepe pinned with a spray of orchids on the shoulder. She waved to Eve and Ollie from the train, her cigarette smoke trailing from scarlet-tipped fingers and curling back into her throat which later sprouted cancer. Immersed in steam, the huge axles muttered and groaned at the train siding. Jean settled into the gleaming wood-panelled dining car, beside her new husband, George Wilson, who 'had money'. She ordered a cocktail, tossing her head at the small desert town and the gossip she was leaving behind.

*   *   *   *

Jean was Ollie's favourite daughter – talented, duplicitous, wayward, laughing. 'She had so much talent,' Eve said, 'and she wasted it.' Jean was so conspicuous that Eve felt invisible. She had grown up pretty and clever but felt non-existent beside scarlet Jean.

Archie drained his family dry with whisky and kept Ollie and his girls needy and wary of his drunken fists. Angry with Ollie and Jean when he couldn't find them after his nightly binge, he hid chocolate under Eve's pillow despite his rage. He can't have been more than sixty when he died. By then, Ollie was long gone from the polished house in the desert and living in Sydney. A young married mother in Broken Hill, Eve found her father's corpse in the house where it had lain for a week in bloating heat.

*   *   *   *

Studying at the conservatorium, Eve learnt to conceive of a career as a concert pianist. As children, when her piano had fallen silent, we felt she should have studied science or gone to medical school and become a doctor. But that was not her path. There had been no money for anything but the music paid for by her aunt, and so she became 'Cousin Eve' at the local radio station instead, where she played the piano with such brio she gained a devoted following, signing autographs on the street: *Best wishes always, Cousin Eve*. She was Cousin Eve on the 'Smilers' Club' at 2BH with 'Uncle Gordon' and 'Gregory the Goldfish', who bubbled remarks through a piece of balloon. At sixteen or seventeen, Eve had a romance she never talked about. The only evidence my sister and I found was a photograph of a man in a double-breasted suit, and we used to believe his name was Fred. At home Eve practised the piano on her mother's rosewood Steinway – the two dragon-headed silver candleholders swung out to light the sheet music – playing Bach, Mozart, Beethoven, Tchaikovsky, Dvorak, Chopin. Her precise, light touch wasted no time on opera. When we were sent to boarding school, Eve insisted my sister and I study piano for five years. This made no difference to us, though, and we became visual artists instead, annoying her considerably. After Eve married Bob, she never played the piano seriously again. If she could not do it with complete brilliance, she would not do it at all.

The fighting mindset of a perfectionist determined to be unhappy.

*   *   *   *

We called Archie 'Flower'. I have a faint memory of a faded old man in a white shirt picking me up to sit me on his shoulder. I thought he was very gentle, but I was two years old. Archibald Campbell Macdougall was from a good family with money, who drank his share of it away along with anything he earned as an agent, and with it all his chances. Eve ignored his drunken rage, or seemed to, and told me that Archie had been a champion cricketer when young and had won a silver cup she later gave to my brother, who played cricket too. 'Archie's mother had lunch sent to the bank for him every day in a horse-drawn wagon,' Eve said. 'She spoiled him.' Eve did not make that mistake with us. 'Understand one thing,' she told my brother when he broke his shoulder at boarding school, and she was called to take him home. 'None of you will ever matter to me the way your father does.'

1936

My oldest niece sent me a photograph of my mother. On the back is written *Off to work*. It is Bebe in 1936, aged nineteen, going to play piano live as 'Cousin Eve'. She told my niece that my father had bought her the long-sleeved, collarless black jacket she was wearing; they had been together since meeting again when she was seventeen. Her dress is dark, cut wide and straight over her chest, the fitted skirt below the knee. She wears kid gloves with big cuffs, high vamped suede shoes, and carries a briefcase and small clutch bag. Her marcel-waved hair is chin-length, parted on the right. She looks straight at the camera, shy, intent, serious, focused but withholding, a face that says, 'Stay away.' She is lovely, this woman who thought she was ugly compared to beautiful, easy Jean.

*   *   *   *

In 1981, Eve's school friend Winsome wrote to her about the fifty-year reunion of their Broken Hill high school. Eve did not attend, and she carefully chose not to remember much of her early life.

30 September

Dear Eve,

It was lovely to hear from Don McGrath at the high school reunion that you knew it was on and had sent cordial messages. We had hearty singing of the high school song, and the Burke, Wills, Parkes and Sturt house songs, and the war cry, do you remember, 'boom jugga boom'. It was strange to see how nicknames not said, or even thought of, for all those years came back in a flash – you would have been Bebe on the spot.

No need to answer this, Eve, I just wanted to share the joy with you.

Love,
Winsome

*   *   *   *

When my father took Eve home for dinner to meet his parents, she was carrying a small, wounded duckling in her coat pocket. I think he decided to marry her then. It was the height of the Depression, with unemployment at almost 30 per cent. Dependent on its exports, Australia's easygoing spirit of 'She'll be right, mate' was rocked to its core, and the seismic tilt buffeted Eve and Bob, trying to start a life together with no money.

When Bob finished high school, he had to forgo a scholarship to university so that there would be enough money for the other five children to go to a private school in Adelaide. He applied for sixty-seven office positions, without success, before going to work for his father while studying accountancy at night. He topped the state and, proud of this achievement, he wrote to his grandfather, signing himself Robert Cotton. The furious response: 'Your name is not Robert Cotton! My name is Robert Cotton. Yours is Robert Carrington Cotton. Kindly sign yourself as such in the future.' This first Robert Cotton had earned the keys to the city of London while working there as a banker, helping trace funds sent secretly from Germany to the Boer War. It was rumoured he had run over the same man twice in one day, once forward and again by backing over him. He drank a bottle of whisky a day and died, aged eighty-eight, when he fell from his roof, having climbed up to fetch his newspaper.

*   *   *   *

When Eve was twenty and Bob twenty-two, they married in Adelaide on 11 November 1937. Tony's mother,

Pauline, was her bridesmaid. The newlyweds sailed for Ceylon (now Sri Lanka) from Adelaide. It was rough crossing the Great Australian Bight and Eve was seasick, but when they reached the islands she found them as enchanting as her childhood dreams of elephants, princes, ivory, gold and flowers.

In a note we found after his death, Bob wrote of a *new world – women in gaily coloured saris with glittering golden headdresses, men with loincloths and caste marks on their foreheads, hair drawn into a knot at the back. November and we were in Colombo, riding in an open car in the Cinnamon Gardens in the moonlight at midnight. The air was filled with flowers and mystery and romance hung around us like an aura. Another night and we walked around the sacred lake at Kandy. There were fireflies in the air and the temple drums were beating.*

They had tea in the famous old colonial hotel, the Galle Face Hotel, in the centre of Colombo, and when they visited my brother in Sri Lanka in 1986, he arranged dinner for them on its terrace, looking out over the sea. The hotel manager, thrilled to learn their honeymoon story, had their names painted on the honour board. In 1937, the honeymooners had travelled to the mountains, seen tea plantations, monkeys and elephants. When they returned to Broken Hill, they had ten shillings left between them and shared a drink of Passiona. In Colombo, Eve had a tailor fashion a dress for her with a bodice of black velvet and an ankle-length skirt of doubled white tulle. My sister and I thought it the most beautiful dress in the world and would take it from her wardrobe to dream over.

*　　　*　　　*　　　*

In 1914 Archibald Campbell Macdougall, a handsome young cricketer, met shy, careful English teacher Olive Harradine from Maitland, and they conceived their first child, Jean. It is shocking to think of my cautious, reserved grandmother allowing herself to be talked into 'going all the way'. They hurried to wed, embarrassed, ashamed, lying about the birth date. Determined to be a perfect wife and mother, Olive followed Archie to the desert town of Broken Hill. Despite all the dust she wiped away, despite her efforts at cooking, turning collars and cuffs, scrimping wherever she could, the marriage was doomed through loneliness, drink, and the desert she hated.

*　　　*　　　*　　　*

When I knew Ollie, she was again the very proper English teacher, correcting our grammar lest we parse a sentence incorrectly, fearful that my sister and I might sit on cold concrete and 'ruin our insides'. She was obsessed with good manners, spelling, grammar and germs. 'Don't sit on the seat,' was her perpetual mantra for public toilets. She seemed a really old lady to me, and wore hats with netting wrapped around her face protecting her from being seen. The fox stole worn around her shoulders had a fierce little face that bit down onto one of its legs to hold it in place, the other three dangled down her back. At bedtime she would sing to my sister and me, 'I was sad because I had no shoes, then I met a man who had no legs.' And would close by repeating her favourite ditty, 'Brown eyes, pickle pies / blue eyes, beauty.' I got the point. We had legs and shoes. I had brown eyes. My sister had blue.

*　　　　*　　　　*　　　　*

Ollie left Archie and the desert to live in a tiny flat in Sydney. Years later, my parents bought her a small house in Greenwich overlooking the water, its garden surrounded by a high wall. Instead of hats with nets, she barricaded herself in this house, behind a front door that opened onto a narrow footpath. She watched the same television channel all the time, not knowing how to change it. What she loved best about the house were the decorative faux wrought-iron railings Jean had cut from black paper and pasted high up on a wall in the narrow front hall. 'She's so talented, she can do anything,' Ollie told Eve. 'Yes,' responded the talented ex-pianist, tight-lipped, the daughter who had just bought her mother a house, her husband a rising political star. Ollie still loved Jean best.

Eve decided that it was not appropriate for us to meet Jean. We were her children. *Hers*. But Jean sent us gifts anyway. One year we were allowed to keep the presents of snowsuits. Mine was red with silver buttons shaped like elephants. I loved it so much that it made Eve furious. I would stamp home in the snow, getting as wet as possible, listening to the silver elephants trumpeting in triumph over my soggy mess. But Eve could no longer hear the magic elephants of her dreams.

*   *   *   *

Horrified to learn that Jean planned to marry an older Catholic man, Ollie's Grandpa Harradine wrote to her from West Maitland. Mixing religions was an unforgivable sin in Australia in those years.

*I will endeavour to complete my letter by
wishing all members of your family a bright,
prosperous, happy new year for 1935. I thank
you most sincerely for your kind remembrances
and gifts. I should very much like to spend a
few days with your family circle, but my health
and surroundings will not permit that. So, I will
content myself with the next best substitute,
namely, correspondence. My own observations
are such, that mixed-religion marriages are
failures so far as happiness and contentment
where the Man and Wife are concerned. But
the head of the Church must interfere if peace
passes out of the family home, as shown by law
court records yearly. It is a question that requires
serious consideration.*

*   *   *   *

*My dear daughter Olly and granddaughter Jean
(with personal Mrs. Wilson),*

*I thank all concerned for the invitation to
attend the wedding of Mr. Wilson to Jean on
Tuesday next – would have felt it a pleasure
to be present in the happy group – but owing
to personal disabilities I regret being unable to*

attend. Nevertheless, though absent, I offer silent prayers to our all-wise God to plead for a happy and prosperous union throughout this life and in the world to come life everlasting.

From,
Grandpa

*   *   *   *

And this same Grandfather Harradine wrote to Eve:

<u>1 May 1935</u>

Dear Grandaughter Bebe,

I'm ashamed to delay any longer a reply to your hearty congratulations on the day of my eighty-third birthday and I thank you for hearty good wishes. I went out to watch the Anzac parade for a short time, the passing processions met with pleasure. It was the same route, for some years I had marched with old comrades, [but they] have passed away and left me to stand alone to remember their comradeship.

From Grandpa
1 Michael St, W. Maitland

Eve remembered her grandfather writing in her auto-graph book when she was ten: '*To here hath been dawn-ing another blue day. Think will thou let it slip useless away?*'

1956

Every Anzac Day at boarding school in Bathurst, it was my duty or honour – I was never sure which – to step from the long line of girls standing formally on parade, in blue serge tunics with long-sleeved white shirts and blue ties, and solemnly recite Binyon's poem 'For the Fallen', the lament that always reduced the nation to tears:

> *They shall not grow old, as we that are left grow old:*
> *Age shall not weary them, nor the years condemn.*
> *At the going down of the sun and in the morning*
> *We will remember them.*

It was my task because I did not weep. I had learnt very early that there was no point.

$$*\qquad*\qquad*\qquad*$$

'You're just like Jean!' my sister hissed at me from the front seat of the car. My mother looked smug. I hated them. They knew nothing about me. Nothing! It wasn't fair. We all knew that Jean was the family scandal, so my sister had insulted me as deeply as she could. I flounced the sheet of hair I was growing as long as possible, despite explicit orders from Eve to keep it short. 'Anne has long hair, you have short,' Eve insisted. I sulked. Jean was not the villain they described. She sent us wonderful presents we were not permitted to enjoy, twinsets with yellow lace flowers I secretly adored but was not allowed to wear.

1948

What Jean wanted now that she was living in New Guinea was to see a bird of paradise in the wild, to watch the males courting in a lek, and stroke their long, luminous apricot flank plumes, emerald breast feathers and paired long black tail-wire feathers. She wanted a bird for her shop, which she had named 'Kumul', after the Tok Pisin word. But to get one, Jean had to find an able male to take her into the jungle, to show her where the birds courted and built their nests. She would have them net and kill one for her. Life was cheap in New Guinea after the war. She would close her shop for a week to make the trip. Getting someone to take her wasn't a problem. There were plenty of single, demobilised males working the mahogany harvest and drinking in the bars of Port Moresby. Choosing the most accomplished was her task, to find the one who would bring the best whisky and be the most rewarding in the tent at the end of the day. She packed her safari jacket and pants, the nylon bra and scanties that were presents from the GIs before they left, as well as a sarong and plenty of beads and silver coins for trading. Jean took her own flask – she wasn't about to wait for a man to produce a swallow to deal with the heat, insects, snakes and spiders. Her ex-husband, George the Catholic, was refusing a divorce, but that hadn't stopped

Jean, who traded the diamond ring and pearls he had given her for a flight in a little prop plane to New Guinea from Brisbane. She settled into a hotel in Port Moresby and then set up a shop, arranging anything that appealed to her – bamboo chairs, baskets, pots, coral and shell necklaces, batiks and silk sarongs – anything that might be bought by Europeans wilting with ennui and dissipation. Jean had always had an eye for the unique; spotting it was one of her talents.

She brushed out her long auburn hair, tangled by humidity, and pouted her lips into a perfect bow to apply more scarlet lipstick. When she saw Larry under the low swinging fan in the bar, she whispered to him in her whisky voice, 'Find me a bird of paradise, Larry.' Who could resist Jean? Not Larry.

Larry was used to getting what he wanted, but so was Jean. Port Moresby was made for her, a rainbow palette of flowers, huge insects, life-threatening wildlife, cannibals and horror stories. Jean flourished in the tropical heat, a hibiscus behind one ear as she smacked a scorpion with a shoe, the desert long gone from her heart.

When she finally held the male bird of paradise, she stroked its brilliant sheen. When it was dead, she plucked its feathers with great delicacy, wrapped them in a bamboo sheath and took them to the local dressmaker, saying, 'Make me a bird-of-paradise hat.'

1958

Aged seventeen, I went to Jean's wedding. Actually, it was just a small cocktail party at my parent's flat in Sydney, with hors d'oeuvres and champagne. Jean arrived with her new husband, laughing, and smiling with her big white teeth. She was smoking and wearing a smart hat with a long stream of bird-of-paradise feathers sweeping down her neck. The black tail wires danced along the shoulders of her blue crepe de Chine dress. Jean and her groom had just come from the registry office. Not really. They were pretending to be married for my grandmother's sake. Why did the sham 'husband' go along with it? Ollie was very happy. Eve agreed to lie to her mother and give the fake reception Jean wanted, even though there was no love lost between them. It was too much. The exact amount Jean always wanted. Eve was acid about it all, but I didn't care. I was wearing a white petticoat with a corded flounce, holding out the full skirt of my new dark green poplin dress. I swirled as I walked, wrapped up in myself. A teenage bird of paradise.

*   *   *   *

While Eve was on her honeymoon in Colombo, looking at elephants and monkeys, her dog Mickey died. Her next dog, Mugsy, was a brownish-black cocker spaniel mix with one front leg. His mother had chewed the other one off when he was a pup. How does that happen? Eve loved Mugsy as deeply as one can only love a dog, as deeply as she had loved Mickey. She kept that unreserved love for animals all her life – for Glennie, the black Scottish terrier, for Sally, the ginger cattle dog, and for Lisa, my dachshund.

When he turned six, my brother's birthday present was a little golden cocker spaniel puppy, whom he called Chips. Chips got distemper, which was fatal then. Eve insisted that my brother, sister, and I sit with her and hold the uncontrollably shaking pup while the vet put him down. We held our hands on him, trembling the way Chips was trembling. One minute he was alive and quivering, the next he was dead. What were we supposed to learn from that? That animals die, that love dies, or that you must do the tough thing when the animal you love needs to die?

Glennie, our clever black Scottish terrier, was kidnapped. He somehow made his way home to us six weeks later, starving, near death, one eye bitten out, in what the vet affirmed was a fight with a fox. Not expected to survive, he was sent to the animal hospital in Sydney. To our intense joy, he eventually recovered and lived to be much older. One day, crossing the road to our house, a car struck him on his blind side. Our aunt found him, and when she came to tell us he was dead, we lay on the floor and howled. My father paced up and down, not knowing what to do. Eve wept.

Sally, the cattle dog given to us by a local farmer because she was 'barren', littered sixty-five pups while she was with us. One pup grew up to become Frazer, the meanest dog on the face of the earth. He was my father's mother's dog, and she fed him raw liver three times a day. 'Poor Frazer looks hungry,' my grandmother Muriel would say, looking at his fat black belly lolling to one side while he lay, panting in the heat. His face was that of my night-mares: black dogs with yellow spots above their eyes, red mouthfuls of teeth, clamouring to kill me. I dreamt that I would hide in the car and wind the windows up so tightly that I slowly smothered to death. Could that really happen? I was smothering myself while dreaming, a sheet wound round my head, but still remember their red mouths, their teeth clamouring just outside the glass.

Frazer would sit outside the kitchen door of my grand-parents' house in Broken Hill in the morning, waiting for the first person to use the outdoor 'dunny'. It was always me, and I would have to walk at his desired slow pace, his bared teeth pressed against my bottom, so avid to bite that his drool ran down my legs. He was balanced right on the edge of kill tolerance. Closing the door of the dunny against him, I would feel a brief respite until I saw the spiders there, flesh-coloured tarantulas the size of a child's hand – not poisonous, though they looked it. I still can't bear the sight of them despite being renamed as harmless 'huntsmen'. I would trek back to the house, clenched rigid with fear, Frazer's teeth again pressed hard to my bottom. Frazer had me under his control. He was a fascist dog. My gran would ask ladies over for afternoon tea, and when they arrived, they would stand terrified at the garden gate while Frazer bared his teeth at them and growled. 'Play puppy, Frazer,' Gran would say, cajoling him, and he would pretend to be a puppy for her sake. Not that anyone trusted this puppy play – too much raw liver. My brother remembers Gran saying, 'I'm worried about Frazer. I hope he's getting enough to eat.'

*   *   *   *

My father's father, our grandfather H.L.C. Cotton, had a room downstairs that was stacked with guns with silver chasing and engraved initials on their stocks used for duck hunting on the randomly blooming waterways around Broken Hill. Fascinated by them, my brother and I would go down to the gunroom as soon as our grandparents went out and take one of the guns to fire off across the desert aiming at all the glorious emptiness. We would pry apart the cartridges, pile the gunpowder into little mounds and throw lighted matches onto them, but the explosions were disappointing. Then we would run back downstairs and clean the long barrel of the gun with brushes and oil. We did this repeatedly and I saved the pellets of shot from the large cartridges in a small tin that once held blackcurrant pastilles my father liked to eat. I would take them back to boarding school and madden the dormitory prefect at night by dropping tiny pieces of metal shot that would roll haphazardly across the wooden floor. I always waited until after the silence bell had rung at nine p.m. Unable to find the culprit, the prefect finally asked to be moved.

Home for the holidays, I continued my incendiary experiments by trying to make a bomb. Eve was sick in bed with flu, so I went to the garage where the liquor was kept, reasoning that alcohol would blow up if I mixed whisky and brandy together and applied heat. I swirled it into the bran duck food to use as a binding agent, cut up my bicycle pump to add to the mix, and brought it into the house. I turned the new electric oven to high, ignoring the flames burning ready to ignite it in the old wood stove nearby, put my bomb in to bake, and went to sit by Eve's bed. After a while she said, 'What is that smell?' 'Nothing,' I replied. 'It's just the bomb I'm making.' I had never seen Eve move so fast as she leapt from bed and raced to the kitchen. She was the only thing that exploded. After that, I forgot about bomb-making, and decided to draw pictures on the wall beside my bed at night and collect cow skulls from the back farm to paint.

II

1941

When I was born, my sister closed her mouth, crossed her eyes, and refused to eat. She ended up in the hospital where Eve had just given birth to me, and where our mother had spent six weeks collared in plaster, aged ten. The nurses tried to feed my sister, the doted-on first-born, tiny mouthfuls of mashed pumpkin and oatmeal. She tightened her young rosebud lips, her head a halo of black curls, and refused. My ears stuck out and I had a small, worried frown, which I still have today. As the second child, I had displaced the firm centre of my sister's universe. Soon after my birth, Eve found her stuffing my mouth with sultanas. I am unsure whether this was an attempt to share her favourite food, or silence me permanently.

*　　　　*　　　　*　　　　*

It was the depths of World War II and America was soon to be surprised out of its complacency by the savagery of the Pearl Harbor attack on 7 December 1941.

Entering the war with the Allies against the Axis pow-
ers, the United States swept Australia with confidence,
money, nylons, cigarettes and chocolates. As the British
withdrew from their colonial empire, in what would
ultimately be a temporary defeat, America helped shield
Australia, and Australians were overwhelmed, bemused
and set on edge by the sudden influx of US soldiers.

*   *   *   *

Once crossed, my sister's eyes stayed that way. She had
amblyopia, 'lazy eye', and wore a small pair of wire-
rimmed glasses with brown paper stuck over one lens,
an attempt to force her eyes straight. She looked puzzled
and unhappy, and my parents were troubled. What could
they do during World War II about a child's eye? A whole
universe – a world and its way of life – was being blown
apart. But a child's eye is a whole universe too.

My father was training to fly for the Royal Australian
Air Force, and the eye exercises he was required to learn
involved repeatedly crossing and uncrossing his eyes.
When I heard about this later, aged four or five, I determined to do them myself, reckoning that they must be
excellent exercises as my father would have had to see
much further from a plane than from the warships where

he had wanted to serve. He had been refused on the grounds of poor eyesight, but I learnt from these exercises and can still spin my eyes with ease to this day.

*   *   *   *

Fainting under a truck she was learning to take apart, Eve discovered she was pregnant with me. She had volunteered to be a truck driver for the war effort. I was born in 1941, and in 1943 Eve, pregnant again, was in despair. How would she cope with a world war, probable invasion by the Japanese, no money and three children, including a cherished firstborn wearing glasses with brown paper over one eye, a child who bumped into things and was unhappy.

In July 1941, when I was three months old, Bob wrote:

> *Most illness hit one like a blow, suddenly and without warning; having a baby is different. It is prepared for, inexorable. The mother knows that on a certain date a child will be born to her – she knows now while a new life is still stirring within her that one day she is going to be very ill and suffer such pain that in its throes the only person she will have any affection for will be the doctor,*

and he only because he brings blessed release. You will see that it is an undertaking for the courageous and not the craven-hearted. Every woman who has had children is braver than any man can be.

1943

With my father posted to the Department of Supply, we moved not long after my brother was born from Broken Hill to the tiny, frosty hill town of Oberon in New South Wales, where Bob was to open a lumber mill for the war effort. I remember standing on the crumbling desert earth of Broken Hill, at the bottom of our garden in long dry grass, the wind whistling in my ears, and all my life that red earth has stayed with me. In Oberon's cold high country, we lived in a boarding house, *Dulce Domum*, while our house was being built during the privations and shortages of war time. Whenever I asked Eve what she recalled from those days, she would shudder with distaste. 'There were flies everywhere, and Dulcie would put fried eggs on the plate with her bare hands!' Nothing could ever be clean enough for Eve. I remember the cracks in the cold, pisé-plastered rooms, the wide verandah, and an old brown draught horse that stood placidly outside for us to sit on. My baby brother sat on the horse too. He laughed a lot. He still does. Placed in his pram outside in the sun, he undid the straps that held him in, fell onto the cement verandah and knocked out his two new front teeth. It took ten years for him to grow two more, but he learnt to whistle through the gap. It took two years to build our house.

*　　　　*　　　　*　　　　*

My father, LAC Robert Cotton #419078, had joined the air force and learnt to fly Avro Anson twin-engine Lockheed reconnaissance bombers that could land in Broken Hill. 'You flew in one with me when you were a baby,' Eve told me. 'I was airsick, Anne was airsick. Over the desert there are huge bumps of air, and my hat flew off my head.' In 1938 Bob had been attached to the Department of Munitions for eighteen months, working in timber supply because his father's company, which he had joined, had shown that an 8×8 local ash pit prop in the mines could outperform a 10×10 pit prop from Oregon in America. After Bob joined the RAAF in 1942, the Department of Supply seconded him from it because he understood the mines and miners of Broken Hill. The excavation of silver, lead and zinc – in one of the largest deposits on earth – was vital to the war effort, particularly to the manufacture of ammunition and aircraft parts. When the United States entered the war after the Japanese bombed Pearl Harbor, the supply of timber pit props from Oregon was interrupted, Bob knew that the miners were a superstitious lot, and that their trust in pit props was vital. Those props were all that saved them from lung-choking cave-ins that could smother their lives. My father's maternal grandfather was a Cornish miner who had married a French woman and travelled to Australia looking for work after she died giving birth to their twin girls. One twin died later but the other, Muriel, a true beauty in every sense, became my grandmother. My father said he learnt much from this 'good quiet man' who worked as a blacksmith in the mines.

Bob had been sent on a walking trip in 1941 by the Department of Supply to search the deep forests of south-eastern New South Wales for hardwood lumber for the mines. Trekking through the countryside, he fell in love with the high bush country of the Blue Mountains and the Oberon plateau, especially the walk from Kanangra Walls, near the Jenolan Caves, through the Burragorang Valley. This valley had a hidden entrance, and it was rumoured that one of the war plans was to drive all the cattle and sheep that could be mustered into the valley and let them loose, preventing the Japanese from finding provisions for their troops when their expected invasion advanced on this almost unguarded island.

Bob found the timber he was looking for in the virgin eucalypt forests that cloaked the slopes of the Blue Mountains. After the war, he would tell us stories about his long treks, and of snaring eels in the creeks to roast over a campfire. He had a gift for poetry, and I imagine this young father reciting Keats or Shelley to himself, or maybe our childhood favourite, W.S. Gilbert's *The Bab Ballads*, whistling as he walked in the pristine bush. I imagine him as young and hopeful because he was. Later, opening the sawmill in Oberon in 1943, he had it up and running in eleven months, and after the war took it up as his first business venture, borrowing a tractor, a wheelbarrow, and a shovel to do so – or so the story goes. After his death, we found some of his writing.

Robert Cotton, January 1941

You will be lying on a ridge top in the mountains, it will be night time, a clear luminous night with the wind softly swaying the trees and near you the edge of another abyss, but a green, carpeted, unfathomable cool mysterious one along whose bottom a tiny stream of cold mountain water that started life as a waterfall hides amongst the ferns, and as the stars above twinkle back your thoughts to you, time is eternal, you are a God, you are Olympus. The morning breaks and you gaze from your lofty fortress over the top of an ocean of crested clouds, down through which you must walk. You plunge into the clouds and

*suspended in their white mist clamber over
the cliff face where it takes an abrupt rocky
collapse to the green valley some thousand feet
below, going down by tortuous zigzag track
your rucksack thumping on your back at the
turns. Miraculously the mist springs to life
and soon you hear the creek whispering beside
you and it seems to speak of adventure, new
lands, new thoughts, and you begin to feel like
a pioneer.*

Riding home again, he wrote:

*I came back to civilisation on top of a load of
wool and lying up there in the sun I can see a
stone, water-worn, with a stream and trout
darting along its sandy bottom, gurgling around
it and as it becomes more distinct, I find myself
a year from now walking with a rucksack on my
back. It is late afternoon, I had been tramping
all day and at last broke out on the end of our
plateau, and there far below, cradled in a cup of
the hills, was tea and sleep. Scrambling down the
mountainside I reached it and after a swim stood
in the orchard, eating apples and strawberries
as they grew.*

And ruminating on his life:

As I stand on this stone it topples and as I try to regain my balance one day returns to me. I had walked all the morning along a plateau and in the distance on either side and could see the edge of the world giving way to nothing before the blue distance of far-off mountains. Coming around a corner tall trees were blacked against white clouds on the edge of the plateau. As I reached the brink far down and away, mile upon mile of sheer forest surrendered eventually to hazy farming land with lakes flashing in the sun. As I gazed the mist rising slowly up from below like a white wraith enveloped me and took away the view, as it did the stone on which I stood seemed to vanish with it leaving me suspended in time.

1949

The vast, hallucinatory landscape of Kanangra Walls
was thirty miles from our farm, and we would lie on our
bellies on the cliff top, trying to find Mount High and
Mighty, Mount Stormbreaker and Mount Cloudmaker.
The sandstone domes we lay on seemed carved like
ancient Aztec heads, peering out into the breathing blue
bush, haunted by myth and legend. We watched waterfalls tangle with rainbows, having just waded squealing
with delight in their icy streams. These waterfalls gave
vivid life to the myth of the traditional people, the Gundungurra, that the part-fish, part-eel Gurangatch and the
tiger quoll Mirrangan had battled so fiercely there that
they had formed the whole gorge (nearly 3000 feet deep)
of the Wollondilly and Coxs rivers. Tiger quolls and rock
wallabies still abounded at Kanangra, the wallabies easy
to spot.

Exploring the sloping cliffs behind the lookout where we
had lain on our bellies, we found an old wooden dance
floor clinging under the lip of a sandstone cave. It reeked
of trysts and unruly passion, of nights twirling to a fiddle
or harmonica, heads so addled with whisky that dancers
fell into the bracken, copulated, and produced the next
generation of invaders.

Not far away were some of the world's oldest caves, the Jenolan Caves. They were terrifying pleasure palaces of starkly lit limestone stalactites and stalagmites, gleaming crystal in the echoing and shadowy dark beside mysterious subterranean waterways. We did not know that this storied dwelling place was inhabited by the Burra Burra people, a group of the Gundungurra Nation, for tens of thousands of years, who thought of these underground rivers as places of healing. After its so-called 'discovery' in 1838 by James Whalan, these people were pushed away by European colonists with stockwhips, guns, horses and sheep in an attempt to subdue this ancient untameable land, and the caves were turned into a tourist site. All we understood when we were there was that there was startling magic at Kanangra and Jenolan; they were places of spirits, ghosts, and majestic beauty that we could barely comprehend, but which took our breath away.

Did Bob clamber down Kanangra's vertiginous, precarious cliffs, rucksack banging on his strong young back, in his search for hardwood lumber to aid the war effort? The known world was being torn apart as I was born into it in 1941. Looking out over the miles of mist-clouded bush, did he feel like a god, lord of all he surveyed, or did he worry about the future? In later

years, he never appeared to look back, but only forward
to where he could climb next.

1944

The house built for Eve in Oberon was painted white with dark blue trim around the windows and window boxes, which spilt matching dark blue lobelia. On her first day at the local school, in 1944, my five-year-old sister set out from this house wearing wire-rimmed glasses with brown paper over one eye. I was so furious with her for leaving that I took a hammer and smashed her favourite china doll with blue glass eyes.

My parents made their final decision about changing my sister's eyesight, and without any explanation put us in brown serge tunics, white shirts and brown ties and drove us to Orange, over bumpy dirt roads that silted our noses with beige dust. The sixty-mile trip took two hours in 1946, and my sister was carsick. We were being taken to a boarding school, Onslow House, near an eye specialist; my sister was not quite seven, I was not yet five. The war was barely over. We had no idea what we were doing in this small Church of England boarding school for country children, and we did not understand that our parents would leave us there. Through the tunnel of time and distance, I still see the darkness, smell the soapy dishwater, cabbage, and furniture polish, remember the lonely night-wet cots and the terrible longing for home.

I resisted being born. 'Two days,' Eve complained, 'and you wouldn't get started.' It was at this boarding school that I began to perfect my talent for stubbornness. Our first meal there was Sunday lunch. Plates of sliced corned silverside the colour of oil spill and shredded cabbage dressed with condensed milk and mustard were put on the table. 'Sit in silence and eat everything on your plate!' we were directed by the teachers. When all were finished but my plate remained untouched, I was kept back to sit alone in the dining room from noon till six p.m., slowly scraping dressing from every piece of food and wiping it on the plate rim. At six p.m., they relented and took away the meal.

The older children held terror raids and would run wildly into our dormitory early in the morning, yelling, 'A pinch and a punch for the first of the month!' They regarded this as tacit permission to beat us. For some reason this always came as a surprise to us. Years later, I met one of the older girls who had been a raider, and she told me I had once pulled a wardrobe down on top of her during an attack.

Twice a week, my sister was taken to the eye specialist to sit in a darkened room and stare into the stereo-optic cups of an eye-exercise machine. Her task was to put a butterfly in a net, a lion into his cage. I was envious of these pictures that only she could see. I imagined them burning like incandescent rainbows. The exercises made her cry. She knew she was different from everyone else, and the other children teased her. She closed tight, rolled herself into a ball like an echidna covered in spikes, and focused inward. I was still trying to under-stand where I was, who I was supposed to be, where to walk, where to stand. 'Don't walk near me,' my sister the echidna commanded, and I would be overcome with an inexorable magnetic thrall, trailing in her wake like detritus after an ocean liner. I didn't understand why she cried, and every night as I put on the pink dressing-gown my mother had knitted me, I hoped that each clear plastic star button I slipped through its loop was a sign I would see her again.

*   *   *   *

It was here that I was shaken awake nightly by a recur-ring nightmare, dreaming I was tucked so tightly into a cream wicker pram I was unable to move. As I struggled to free myself, my family stood beside me mute while the ground between us ruptured with tectonic shudders into bottomless crevasses roiling with ochre mud. Each spasm of the earth pushed my family further from me, until they disappeared from my sight. In time I chose to make them disappear, swimming away from home into another hemisphere, crammed into the tight aluminium tube of an airliner.

*   *   *   *

When my sister went to hospital for her eye operation, it was kept secret from me. I was taken to the local country fair as a distraction, the only child from our school to go. I asked to buy her a present and chose a pinwheel of gaudy coloured plastic that fluttered from its fastening to a small wooden dowel. The teachers decided to buy more for the children left at school and, riding back on the bus, I held all the pinwheels out the window, hypnotised by the colours that spun into rainbows. I took this pinwheel to my sister, who was sitting up in a hospital bed, a white gauze bandage wrapped around her head, covering her eyes. I was dumbstruck by the belief that her head had been sawn in half, and the two halves stuck back together. She was drawing blind with a pencil on a small pad. 'Is the chimney on the roof? Is the roof on the house? Is the cat on the chair?' she asked. Mutely, I offered her the turquoise and pink pinwheel she could not see, and then agreed with anything she asked. I imagined that a head sliced in half then put back together must be truly uncomfortable. During surgery, the lazy eye muscle had been cut and her eyes straightened. She had to continue the eye exercises in a darkened room, and she continued to ignore me. My sister the echidna retreated into books, invisible walled rooms of silence, where words made pictures that fleshed out into complete worlds that only she could live in, her alternate universe.

* * * *

Saturday mornings were for hair washing. The headmistress's beautiful daughter would hold me, tip my head back over the laundry sink, and sing, 'I'm going to wash that man right out of my hair.' It was my favourite time of week. On Saturday afternoons we watched her in silent adoration stretched out on the lawn in the sun, fresh mint rubbed on her legs to keep flies away. We were in awe of the red nail polish on her fingers and toes, and the artful line drawn with an eyebrow pencil up the back of her calves to simulate stocking seams when she went out at night. She seemed the essence of glamour. It was 1946, and nylon stockings were rare as diamonds. The Yankee influx of chocolates, cigarettes and nylons had not made it up the 160 miles over the Blue Mountains from Sydney to Orange.

Some nights, a little boy three years older than me would take me on his knees and sing to me, 'You are my sunshine, my only sunshine.' It comforted me until he sang the rest of the song: 'The other night, dear, as I lay dreaming/I dreamt I held you in my arms/when I awoke, dear, I was mistaken/so I hung my head and I cried.' I would feel tears begin but knew better than to let them run down my face. Tears would change nothing, and we would still be far from home.

One afternoon, I fell against the enamel tub in the bathroom. One of the female staff, not a teacher, bathed and dressed me in my new pink rayon pyjamas and knitted pink dressing-gown and took me in a taxi to a doctor. I remember lying on a big bed in a darkened room. There was a white sheet tucked tightly over the bed. The doctor, a man wearing a white coat and glasses, pulled down the sheet, then my pyjamas, and proceeded to do unbearable damage to me. After that I remembered nothing, until years later I understood what he had done, and that I would never escape it.

*   *   *   *

Back at the boarding school, I began to cough in the night. My chest hurt and I coughed so hard I woke in a big, congealed pool of vomit. I had pertussis, whooping cough. My sister and I were taken away from the school. Running a high fever, I remembered nothing, my brain having gone to sleep. I woke one day in a hotel bed near Manly Beach in Sydney. My pink dressing-gown was there, as well as raspberry-flavoured cough medicine and all the books of paper dolls I could want. I cut the dolls from their cardboard covers and dressed them in the clothing printed inside. The dresses fastened with white tabs that folded over the one-dimensional dolls. I coughed and coughed but I was happy. My mother and father, my sister the echidna, with eyes that no longer crossed, and my younger brother were all there. When I was almost well again, my brother and I discovered the lift and rode it up and down all day, finding to our delight that we could spit off the hotel roof at beer drinkers on the pavement below, nailing them with tiny drops of saliva.

*　　　　*　　　　*　　　　*

My parents built three houses: the first in Broken Hill, the second in Oberon and the third at our farm, four miles outside the town of Oberon. At the second house, on Jenolan Street, we had two rams called George and Cheeky, two dogs and two white Muscovy ducks. Our cousin Tony lived three houses down and was always with us. We would feed sour Kentish cherries from the two trees in the back garden to the ducks, who would roll them back and forth in their bills and then spit the pips out one side. Eve liked to eat the ducks' eggs, but I hated them. All eggs – even the fresh ones from the Nichols family, who raised hens just down the road – were stored in waterglass in a laundry tub. When my mother told me to get some, I would have to put my hand into the gelid slime and pull them out. Meanwhile, the small refrigerator fuelled by kerosene whined and wheezed on the narrow back porch, keeping meat cold and leaking water over a drip tray.

When my mother went out one day for afternoon tea, my brother and I half-filled the watering cans and set cement in them so that when covered with water they would seem easy to pick up instead of pounds of inexplicable weight. Then I explained to him that 'all ducks had ponds', and with a burst of enthusiasm, we dug a big round pond in a patch of lawn behind the garage, filled it with the hose and slopped happily in the mud. I'm not sure how the ducks felt about their pond, but giddy with the gooey mess, we made mud pies and threw them at the white garage walls to see if they would stick.

Looking for trouble one winter afternoon, my sister, my brother, Tony, Rob's friend Squeak, who lived in the house behind us, and I climbed to the top of the hill where a huge old neglected concrete water tank stood. My brother, Robert, and Tony climbed the tree beside it to inspect the water, which was so green with slime that we decided it would be a public service to let it out. Repeatedly bashing the outlet pipe with rocks, we finally broke through and water began to trickle out, then flow quite fast. We all yelled excitedly, and Tony said, 'Someone go see how much water has gone out.' Rob climbed the tree again and crawled out along a branch. But it cracked under his weight, and he fell in with a huge splash. The concrete tank had no ladder inside or out and was over ten feet tall. The weather was freezing cold, and my brother was wearing a knitted wool balaclava to protect his ears, which had nearly killed him with infected mastoids. Now, there was silence. Panicked, Squeak called out, 'Robert, are you dead?' With a hiss of fury, Rob yelled back, 'YES!' The water was deep enough to break his fall, but not deep enough to drown in. We had to get him out. Tony picked up a fallen branch, climbed the tree and, while we all held onto him, lowered it to Rob, who held on tightly as we pulled him out over the top of the concrete tank. He was wet, furious, and covered in green slime. My sister and I ran home with him, repeating the whole way, 'Boy, you are in for it! You are so going to get into trouble!' Eve was livid. She bathed him in scalding water, stuffed 'magic wool' in his ears, fastened that mysterious pink cotton batting – supposed to be a potent instrument of healing – inside a woollen singlet with safety pins, and put him to bed with a hot water bottle in the middle of the afternoon. He was mortified. But for Eve, he was the son who had nearly died from infected mastoids and rheumatic fever when she was in Queensland, picking up her drunken mess of a sister. He had been taken to hospital, and the archbishop of Queensland came to pray over him. He still remembers the big mitre on his head and the ring he was allowed to play with.

*   *   *   *

At two years old, my brother was very susceptible to my experiments. One day I took him to where the house paint was stored under the tank stand, which collected rainwater near the strawberry bed in the back garden. It was 1945, and America was about to drop the atom bombs *Little Boy* on Hiroshima and *Fat Man* on Nagasaki. Australia seemed far away from these events. Despite rationing, Eve had managed to get some grey wool flannel made into matching boilersuits for my brother and me that zipped up the front in emulation of Winston Churchill, Australia's unquestioned hero at that time. Having washed and dressed us in these, Eve left us briefly unattended to primp for a tea party. I took my brother to the tank stand, pried the lids off the paint cans, removed the thick skin of clotted paint on top and began to paint him. He was patient and cooperative, standing quietly smiling, but then he has an even temperament to this day. I can't remember my mother's reaction – young Eve from Broken Hill, learning to settle down in this small, cold country town where all behaviour was scrutinised by the locals. She must have beaten me with a hairbrush, but I only remember the pleasure of the paint, and how it felt to flatten my brother's hair with it, to twirl the brush in the concave shell of his ear. How did she clean us, remove the oil paint from his ears and hair? Is that why she sent me away to school with my sister before I had turned five? When I was thirty, I asked her why she had sent me too and she replied, 'Oh, frankly, we sacrificed you.'

1949

After my bout of whooping cough and subsequent release from boarding school, my sister and I were sent to the local Oberon school instead. We had a wonderful teacher, Geoff Spinney, who taught all classes in one big room heated with a wood stove, on which we toasted our sandwiches. He always wore a suit and tie, and I vividly remember a poem he recited to us – Hilaire Belloc's 'Tarantella':

> *Do you remember an Inn,*
> *Miranda?*
> *Do you remember an Inn? ...*
> *And the fleas that tease in the High Pyrenees*
> *And the wine that tasted of tar? ...*
> *Do you remember an Inn?*

Although I was only eight years old, I have never forgotten the sound of his yearning. Did he ever reach the Pyrenees and the European civilisation of his dreams? Mr Spinney taught our class a game called 'Parliament', which we would enact with great force and vigour. When I came home from school one day, I told my mother, 'We had Parliament today, and Mr Spinney had his head out the window and his face was red.' Eve replied, 'He was laughing.'

When my parents gave a party, my sister and I were allowed to sit in little chairs in the doorway of our bedroom to watch the adults drink and chat, while my mother played dance tunes on the piano. I was entranced by her fluid fingers running up and down the white keys, summoning music to flow out and enchant the room. In the laundry, the town doctor, Lance Robey, who took out my tonsils, would shuck fresh oysters shipped in muddy sacks on the train from Queensland that stopped nearby at Tarana. He was helped by Mr Osborne, the local chemist, whose life would end with savage abruptness. The adults seemed to undergo a mysterious change at the party, laughing over oysters and beer, but Mr Spinney, careful in his suit and tie, remained dreaming of Spain. We would go to bed listening to the mirth and chatter outside our small door.

Darryl Cunningham was a local boy our age who hunted for rabbits with his .22 rifle. He could not have been more than eight when he was found dead one winter afternoon on a cold hillside. We never found out how. Was it a mistake? Were there dead rabbits with him? Did he trip or did he mean to do it? Rabbits and turkeys were hung on hooks in a large concrete bunker, a big freezer dug under a hill, run by the local butcher. Eve would go there to buy ducks or turkeys and if I were with her, I would smell the dried, furry pelts, think of Darryl, and wish we had told him how much we liked him.

During school recess we played 'poison base', racing back and forth as boys tried to tag girls and vice versa. One day I smacked hard into the Armstrong boy and bit through both my lips. For weeks, they flaked off in brown strips as if I had just eaten a meat pie. When he brought me an ice cream cone in an apologetic approach, I threw it on the floor. The other children would also 'play doctor', but I refused. I had learnt the hard way what 'playing doctor' could mean. While they examined each other at recess, I built complicated houses fashioned from piles of pine needles that I had raked into thin walls, complete with doorways, windows, entrances and exits.

1954

After we moved to the farm, our cousin Tony would often come to stay. He was our best friend. 'I just love that boy,' his aunt Eve would say of him. 'No matter how many times you bat him down, he bounces right back up, grinning.' Rob, Tony and I were inseparable, and we loved Tony as only connected children can love, a love that lasts a lifetime. We would tease the hens at the farm manager's house on top of the hill when he had left us briefly in charge of feeding them, building nests in the hay barn and shoving them in beak-first, demanding, 'Go lay an egg!' When huge thunderstorms broke, Tony, Rob and I would run outside to dance in the pelting bullets of rain. Eve loved thunderstorms – they relaxed something taut in her, rain a panacea for a desert child. Despite the lightning flashing and striking all round us, Eve would laugh encouragement. She always wanted to join in, but the rain would have messed up her hair.

During summer we would run barefoot down the hill through hay as tall as we were, delighted by the terror of possible imminent death from poisonous snakes. We would scramble up the old cherry trees and sit in their branches, eating crimson and pale pink cherries. Pink and grey galahs ate beside us. Tony, Rob and I would climb the pea-vine stack and throw sticks at the solitary Hereford bull until he grew surly enough to chase us. We would then leap onto the tractor, my brother driving at top speed with Tony and I half spilling off the trailer and would just make it out the gate before the bull reached us. When the hay was harvested, we would ride around the paddocks, under the full moon. I would sit on the baler and help push out bales tied with green twine, and then Rob and Tony would stack them. Later, we would pile into the back of the truck yelling songs as loudly as possible as we drove through the bush on dusty country roads.

When we drove from Oberon to the tiny crossroads named Titania, I would see eagles that had been shot by farmers and strung up by their feet, hanging head down from the wire fences like bizarre stage props in a macabre *Midsummer Night's Dream*. The farmers believed the eagles killed the sheep and perhaps they did. Bob, who was expanding his hold on the land, now owned two farms. At the back farm, where my father's youngest sister and her husband, our aunt and uncle, lived, I caught little painted burrowing frogs that swam in the small creek under the footbridge or threw sticks into the dam. One winter's day, Rob dared Tony to walk out onto its ice. It was so thin he fell in. What did this tell us about what lay ahead? That Tony would take any dare and fall?

*   *   *   *

Italian prisoners of war were interned in the district in the 1940s, and they cheerfully made vodka from potatoes. They gave my father a bottle of it, which he kept for so long that he offered my husband a glass of it nearly forty years later. Being a POW was still imprisonment and it was rough, but the Italians told him that they preferred being in Australia and far away from a maddened Europe. Many settled in Australia eventually and changed the whole picture of 'everything closed on weekends', with little cafes that sold wonderful coffee and pastries. They brought a sense of worldly culture but were resented; this was 'White Australia', and its citizens detested outsiders of any other colour or race. But the coffee slowly brewed out some of the rage, and by the time I went to university, coffee shops were the heart of beatnik sophistication. I spent most of my university years in those cafes, drinking coffee, wearing black stockings, skipping lectures, and learning to smoke with a long telescoping cigarette holder.

In my fresher year at Women's College at Sydney University, I contracted meningitis. With my temperature rising, a violent headache splitting my skull into shards I descended swiftly into delirium. My roommates carried me to the quarters of the principal, Doreen Langley, who was so decent that she rose every three hours in the night to sponge me down and listen to my raving nightmares. I tried to explain to her the savage pain attacking my spine: 'I am a shellfish and they have taken away my shell.' In an act of delirious cunning, I crawled to the bottom of the bed and hid beneath the covers to escape the doctor. I stayed in her quarters for several weeks, watched over by medical students. My sister came to see me, a worried frown on her face, but I would not let her tell Bob and Eve what had happened. When they were finally informed, they visited with a certain level of gaiety, having just won a bet at the Melbourne Cup. I had made it through, so it was back to business.

In my year at Women's College, I used to visit an old woman who lived on a lane nicknamed Blood Alley that led briefly between the college and Newtown's high street. I did the weekly shopping for her which always comprised a whole sheep's head wrapped in bloody butcher's paper and not much more. She lived in one dark, cluttered room that opened directly onto a strip of pavement less than two feet wide. One night, walking up the alley to join my friends, a man, a stranger, drove his car wildly at me, trying to smash me into the wall, reversing three times to crush me against the bricks. I dodged the car and ran breathless and panting onto the bus, where my friends were waiting. 'Why?' they asked. 'I don't know why,' I replied.

*   *   *   *

In the three-hour exams at Sydney University for the 'Arts' course I was taking, though no art was included, I wrote long essays explaining what I thought was wrong with the questions. Not what was asked for. I was not about to spit back information already chewed and lobbed into our supposedly open beaks. But then, I had spent most of my time in Manning coffee house, eating apple strudel with cream, reading detective novels and not the required texts. I had been furious with my father exercising his authority over me in determined opposition to art school, declaring artists immoral lechers and degenerates who would attempt to seduce me. He felt the same way about advertising, my next suggestion, and successfully landed me at Women's College, his idea of the proper course for a young lady. But after a year of partying, I rebelled at the whole system of learning and told my mother that I didn't like my father or the university. 'Then leave!' she said coldly, and I did, dropping out and

going to work for the dean of the medical college at St
Vincent's Hospital.

Mistaking me in my white uniform for a medical student,
the doctor would take me on his rounds. I still remember the moans of a female patient thrashing wildly in the
hospital bed as she tore off all her clothes, and a small
boy who was covered in savage burns. The male medical
students seemed to exist solely to sexually harass me. I
eventually got my revenge during their final exams, when
they asked to be excused to go to the bathroom. Serene
in my white uniform at the supervisor's desk on the dais,
I replied, 'You may be excused, but you may not return.'
They were stunned into horrified consternation, having
planned to look up the answers on their bathroom break.

In the specimen lab, I drew excised cancers with coloured
pencil and watercolours, turning their lovely anemones
of deadly flesh into slides for lecture presentations.
After work, I would make my way back to a shared flat in
King's Cross, nose deep in a book, dodging the habitual
drunks spitting and brawling outside the pubs before
closing time.

At night, I went to drawing classes at East Sydney Tech,
the leading art school at the time, where I learnt to draw

three buckets on their sides in perspective, with the requisite academic patterns of shading. But the academic approach bored me and despite Eve's displeasure at the idea of me learning to paint, I found real inspiration in the classes I had slipped out at night for at the Women's College, life classes. I continued to draw from life, and these sessions pointed me towards my future. Had I stayed, I might be living where I once walked, going to the shops for vegetables, bread, and meat, giving brunches in a sunny patio, having affairs with friends' husbands, and living with regret and the buzz of cicadas. But instead, I found a way to leave.

III

1968

Korea was a struggle from the beginning. A naïve, isolated Australian, previously exposed only to New Zealand and hostage to European culture, I arrived as a junior diplomat's wife to a country deep in the throes of the Cold War. Reputed to be only five minutes' flight from North Korea, under curfew and penned into a foreigners' compound in a land that to outward appearances was completely riven by poverty, I felt as if I had landed in a far earlier century. I had never seen such abject need, nor such pockets of reclusive wealth. Never been witness to such a scale of bribery and corruption. 'Import a Mercedes for me. You will be well compensated for it,' was a routine request for diplomats. Nothing could have been further from the easygoing Australia I was accustomed to. Further, I came with the attitude of the late 1960s and its Vietnam War protests, miniskirts and free love. Love and protest weren't an option for a tightly regulated diplomat's wife, but I was determined that if skirts were miniscule in the Western world, then I would bring them to South Korea. I shortened my skirts until half my thighs were bare and was labelled '*La Mini Skirt*' by the French ambassador's wife. Dignitaries would glance askance at my bare legs as we sat in his residence that we called the Blue Palace, waiting for President Park Chung Hee to greet us. He was a repressive military dictator, but when he shook my hand, he just smiled like a country farmer. He offered my son, Tim, and me a ride on his plane to Australia, to accompany him on his trip there. I was aching for home, longing for my feet to touch its soil again. My diplomat husband was stunned when I turned down the president's offer, having thought it a good idea, but I imagined that the price for such a favour would entail quite a bit more than a Mercedes. The Parks were shot in the '70s – his wife in 1974, and the president in 1979 – but by then I was long gone from the 'Land of the Morning Calm', and living in New York.

I did not understand Korea, aghast at the frozen winters of the harsh northern latitude, at a cold so intense I thought my face would crack and fall off. I was stunned by inertia during summers so hot every cell felt drowned in ennui and sweat. I hated being stared at whenever I was in public, hated my son being pinched and pulled by people amazed by his blond hair, hated the crowds that clustered around the car whenever we were driven to the countryside. Unable to find menstruation pads in the department store in downtown Seoul, I could not understand what Korean women used and had no one to ask, so had Tampax sent in the diplomatic bag from Tokyo.

As a third-secretary's wife, it was assumed I would have a modest demeanour and join the coffee mornings where diplomats' wives rolled bandages for charity. But marriage made my spirit itch and instead of dressing well and giving sophisticated dinners of duck a l'Orange or roast pheasant as recommended by Eve, I wrote art criticism for *The Korea Times* and designed clothes for Julia Lee's fashion business. Julia was an American married to the last Korean prince, Yi Ku. Even though Yi Ku was the only child of Yi Un, Korea was now a republic and princes didn't matter very much. Julia was a lively modern woman and Yi Ku a gentle soul. They lived in a residential compound called *Nakseonjae* in *Changdeokgung*, one of Seoul's five royal palaces. We would eat there, sitting on cushions on the floor of the 'moon room' and watch its orb blaze through the rounded opening framed as its echo. Eve approved of me dining in a palace and attending lavish galas but thought that working while a diplomat's wife was simply 'not done'.

It was a life of privilege and deprivation, and I was as disenchanted with the world as it seemed to be with me.

I was overwhelmed by the rank smell of kimchi in the stifling heat of the cabs I took to work. If I was unable to get one home, I would walk the long road back to the compound, feeling determinedly independent and Australian. On more than a few occasions, I was struck by stones thrown to indicate contempt for Western women, considered lower than prostitutes because, as it was explained to me, 'A prostitute has a function, but a Western woman has no function.'

I tried learning taekwondo, which in Korean means 'the art of kicking and punching'. My instructor, who apparently did not believe in washing his *dobok* uniform and stank of sweat and kimchi, informed me in one class, 'You woman! You, number ten!' Crowing loudly, he said, 'I man! I number one!' I was so furious with him I broke my toe practising the balled foot *chagi* kick to his chest and remained so enraged that I continued the lesson despite the fact that we both knew my toe was broken. 'You man! You, number ten!' my toe told him. We had both broken the five rules of taekwondo: courtesy, integrity, perseverance, self-control and indomitable spirit. I had the stubborn spirit part down but we both lacked the courtesy.

JUDY COTTON

Buying rice one summer's day in the quixotic Korean
market, the women squatting over the boiling brass pans
of offal cackled and jeered at me from a narrow alley. I
had reached my limit with Korea when a sudden rain
squall soaked through my paper bag of rice, causing it to
break and the grain to spill all over the stones, mud and
shit. The women howled with laughter, but then busily
scraped up every grain of rice and put them in another
bag, before bowing and giving it to me, which was how
I learnt something of what rice was worth, and that I
understood nothing. What would Eve have done? She
would have bowed graciously in return and given them
money. I tried to do that, but my spirit was raw and the
effort showed.

As only American generals could, one of them decided I
should draw Freedom House for him. It was in the DMZ
and he had me driven the thirty miles there to near the
38th parallel with a full military guard. I stood in the middle of the strangely lush no-man's-land that separated the
two Koreas. It was 160 miles long by 2.5 miles wide and
abundant with growth and pheasant, because it had not
been hungrily picked clean for food or sticks of wood
used for fuel. I drew the building while surrounded on
four sides by soldiers holding rifles. North Korean guards
watched me steadily through binoculars.

Hiking in the hills on winter afternoons, we would sometimes stumble into old foxholes, remnants of the Korean War, and emerge from the woods above rice paddies quilted with beige tufts of stubble, to see smoke coil in grey curls from the little cottages where fires had been newly lit under *ondol* floors. The floors were hard, but the rice paper covering them had been lacquered and heated so many times they had become the colour of amber. If we stayed for a night at a local house used as an inn, a quilt would be spread for us to sleep on, and in the morning, we would be greeted with winter root kimchi, rice, and hot barley tea, not understanding that this was a feast.

I came home one night from yet another pointless cocktail party to find my young son alone in the darkened house. Miss Cho, our maid, was missing. A few hours later she returned, carrying her twenty-year-old son, a ragged mess of starved bone and skin. He had been arrested with other students demonstrating against the oppressive dictatorship of Park Chung Hee. Thrown into a crowded cell, he lay for months on the freezing cement floor with almost no food or water. We tried every means possible for the embassy to free him, but to no avail. Embassies had no pull with Korean jailers. 'Tonight was the night they would take the bribe,' Miss Cho explained weeping as she held her son and carried him to her quarters. He stayed there with us from then on, but he never recovered. Occasionally I would see his pale wraith-like form drifting around the garden. He was broken.

General Bonesteel, the commander-in-chief of US and UN forces in Korea, chose Tim and me to light the Christmas tree with him at the American compound. There, in front of the rows of polished steel helmets of the guard of honour, as well as the resident Americans, we threw the switch and the tree lit up. Everything was incongruous. Where were the family Christmases that Eve presided over with such precision, the temperature in the high nineties, the house aromatic with resin from a perfectly decorated giant pine tree, gifts piled underneath it, hot mince pies, family visits, roast turkey and flaming plum pudding, where Ollie once mistakenly ate the silver shilling hidden in her slice. 'Got anything yet, dear?' Eve enquired rather anxiously, to see if Ollie had found it. 'No,' Ollie replied, smiling, not having understood that she was about to make change. Christmas was supposed to be hot and full of noisy family – not lonely and surrounded by strangers in a frozen land covered in snow.

I came to relish Mary's Alley, a treasure-trove of lacquered antique chests and carved jade, though there was nothing there that I could afford. Showing a visiting dignitary around one day while wearing sandals in the summer heat, I stepped into a steaming pile of human shit to the ineffable delight of the watching urchins. I cleaned it off with my handkerchief, beckoned to the one laughing the hardest, and then gave it to him.

We washed all fruit and vegetables in bleach, but even so I contracted amoebic dysentery and ended up in the American military hospital. Staggering out with a packet of pills, I stood, wobbling and queasy, puzzling over how to get a taxi, when a black car pulled up with my resourceful five-year-old son in it. He had commandeered an embassy car and arrived to take me home. I lay down under cold towels and wondered how to escape.

Invited to the American compound to watch *The Graduate* with friends, I realised as the movie unreeled that if I continued as a married woman in this way of life, there was a fair chance I might one day become a Mrs Robinson, another version of Jean. This was not an option I was prepared to accept. Later, two blue airmail letters arrived from Australia a few weeks apart that led me to the decision to divorce.

1969

'She's my daughter! She's okay!' yelled my father, the honourable senator from Australia, at the Japanese immigration officers who were preventing me from leaving through Tokyo airport's departure gate. 'It's okay, Dad,' I said, 'I just have to write them a letter of apology for overstaying my visa, then they'll let me through.' But Bob kept thrusting his gold senate identification fob at them, repeating, 'She's okay! She's okay!' Eve and Bob were dragging me from freedom in Japan back to my broken marriage in Korea; they wanted to see the wreckage for themselves. People like us did not divorce. The question, really, was why I agreed to go with them. But Eve would not be placated any other way and, after seeing the fractured mess that was my domestic life, they left me stranded and penniless in Korea in the hope that it would force me to stay married and not embarrass them. But, like Jean, I sold my jewellery and, taking my son, returned to Tokyo.

In my letter to the Japanese passport authorities, I had churned out fulsome praise for the country's culture and aesthetic, which had so absorbed me I had not realised my visa was overdue. I was not lying, I was deeply under its spell, in love with the rolls of indigo and white cotton *yukata* cloth in markets that offered every imaginable pattern, ones which could simultaneously differ from each other and yet cohere; with *sumi-e* brush painting on scrolls; with soba, sushi and yakitori stalls; the bowing welcome of *'Irasshaimase!'* customers received upon opening sliding *shōji* doors of restaurants. I was hypnotised by the haunting lament of the man selling roasted sweet potatoes from a handcart as he sang out his wares – *'Yakiimo!'* – which floated down the winter night streets in Harajuku, where I lived in two tiny tatami rooms. Later, Harajuku would become famous for its youth culture, but then it was only beginning.

Escaping from my marriage and life in South Korea, I found a strange peace in Japan. Maybe it was because I could live at last beyond the rules and judgements of diplomatic life and marriage. But it was more than that. Something about Japan spoke to a place deep in my spirit. I was captivated by it, the repetition and symmetry of the old wooden houses, where only rectangles of mulberry paper in wood-lath *shōji* separated them from the street. I was enchanted to sit cross-legged at sumo matches, the national sport, and bet with friends on which giant wrestler, naked except for a black loincloth (*mawashi*), would manoeuvre his opponent with strangely graceful movements over the *dohyō*, the circular boundary ring, having thrown salt for ritual purification under floodlights and banners. This was an art form, and nothing could have been further from the bruising boxing matches I had watched as a child in the Australian bush, all bad-luck losers with bloody noses, reeling on the ropes, a bucket of cold water tossed over them.

I loved the elbowing churn of crowds in Tokyo. In Japan one did not exist until one had been formally introduced. Routinely I would repeat '*Sumimasen*' ('Excuse me') when continually bumped into, and was delighted by the intense politeness with which I was greeted when finally introduced to someone and been seen to exist; I had even begun to bow instinctively when answering the phone with, '*Moshi moshi!*' I loved the ancient, polished ritual and strangely harsh music of classical kabuki theatre. In one performance, the famous kabuki master Ichikawa Ennosuke – renowned for performing in mid-air while held by strings – flew over my head while wearing dramatic colourful robes and hissing with a long red tongue, as I sat in the audience, stunned. During the interval, I was taken by my friend Juliet to sit formally in his tatami dressing room and drink green tea. He gave us face prints by pressing a white cloth against his demon makeup, and gently signed them.

I loved the cleanliness, the fact that I was a *gaijin*, a foreigner, and would never be anything else. Japan was civilised and it suited me well to be 'other', an Australian who had found a place where not fitting in was the best fit. *'Mō sukoshi ōkiino onegaishimasu.'* 'Larger, please,' I would plead, struggling to fit into men's shirts in department stores while the salesgirls collapsed in delighted giggles.

At night I taught English to businessmen, whose favourite joke was for one or another of them to ask me to marry them. They were inordinately delighted by my response of, 'Thank you, but no thank you,' which reduced them to red-faced hilarity each week. I handled English correspondence for a gallery by day and illustrated a book of South Korean birds on weekends. A 1960s feminist, I was against child support and could pay my bills at month's end, but go no further. I had chosen to become a single mother before I realised what that entailed.

Living as I did on the Japanese economy and no longer a 'wealthy foreigner' in an enclave, I was given a form of acceptance. Quite often a local housewife wearing a *'mama san,'* the classic Japanese housewife apron, would arrive at my door, and offer me in carefully folded hands two of the gyoza she had made for dinner. I would reciprocate with slices of French bread and honey from the bakery DonQ, French culture being a particular Japanese obsession.

My son went to an international school, Nishimachi, and would be picked up at three p.m. by our rather hapless maid, Miki San, who seemed to spend the bulk of her time making ikebana arrangements. 'Time for Tim to come in for his bath, Miki San,' I said on the phone one afternoon from the gallery, where I worked until six p.m. She replied, terrified, 'I can't find him!' Hours later, when I had become as unglued as is possible for a *gaijin* mother with her six-year-old son missing in the vast, complex city of Tokyo, he came whistling back up the steps to the apartment. He had gone with the young Irish man who lived nearby to see Shibuya. It had seemed like a good idea to him. I screamed so violently at him that the Irish man ran away in terror. It did not deter my son, though, who disappeared again three weeks later when I was shopping with friends at his favourite toy store, Kiddyland. He knew his way around. What was my problem?

We spent May 5th Festival, Boys' Day – *Tango no Sekku* – at the gallery owner's house in a bamboo forest, flying carp-shaped kites, *koinobori,* adapted from the Chinese legend that held that a carp swims upstream, becomes a dragon and flies to heaven. Japanese culture evolved from Korean and Chinese cultures, and now the way the wind-sock blew made it look as if it were swimming in the air.

Sometimes I would see Mount Fuji standing clear like Hokusai's print 'Gaifu Kaisei' ('Fine Wind, Clear Morning'), smog and mist absent, and vow to climb it along with other pilgrims, but the time never came. Occasionally I was a guest in a traditional red-stained house of wood and paper *shōji* in Nikko, where the bamboo bowed down under the weight of snow. In the freezing evenings spent in the *shōji* house, I soaked in its ancient *ofuro*, a bathtub so old its small oval of wood felt like satin against one's skin. Then I would dress in a cotton *yukata*, the kimono used for sleeping, layer a woollen kimono over it, eat tempura-fried chry-santhemum blossoms and drink sake with the hosts before snuggling under heavy quilts in a bedroom so cold one's breath hung white in the air. I learnt to negotiate earthquakes when tatami floors slid like jelly and learnt the etiquette of bath houses: how to crouch by the tap just above the tiled floor, scrub myself with a small cloth then rinse with buckets of cold water, before daring to immerse myself in the steaming pool, with a bow of my head under the steely gaze of the

local women checking to ensure that I did not trans-
gress the proper procedure.

One long summer weekend, my son and I were on holiday with my lover beside the ocean at the Izu Peninsula
when we were served crab in our room for dinner after
the *ofuro*. We realised the large red crustacean crouching
on the plate was kin with those that wandered near the
sewage outlets spilling into that same ocean. Loss of face
was an imminent problem if we did not eat the meal, so
we buried it under the cherry tree in the small garden
behind the pavilion and left the owners to wonder how
gaijin could eat crab shell.

The small, tight foreign community took me under its
wing. Juliet, a friend at the British embassy, acted as a
loving godmother to my son, and rescued me when ill
health struck hard. At the embassy I met Prince William
of Gloucester – grandson of King George V – who decided
he had to feed a poor colonial some steak, so took me
to the Okura Hotel to dine, where we talked about our
fathers' unrealistic expectations of us. (He died in 1972,
aged thirty, when his plane flew into a tree shortly after
take-off.) I was at his house when Princess Margaret came
to inspect his gorgeous Hungarian lover, ZsuZui. 'I see
your point,' she said to him, 'but she won't do!' Later,

William and ZsuZui took me dancing at Mugen, the hot nightclub where go-go girls danced all night in glass booths beside the dance floor. Exiting after midnight, we saw the most beautiful gender-fluid geisha, whose services were probably for sale, made up like those in the *ukiyo-e* woodblock prints, with white faces and customary black wigs, baring above their kimonos that most erogenous zone, the powdered nape of their necks.

*   *   *   *

At night I painted on rice-paper panels on the floor and held a show of my work at the Frannell Gallery. Japanese artists befriended me and took me to see the print shops that handled the different stages of making traditional *ukiyo-e* woodblocks, so that I could learn how each carved cherry-block piece dovetailed over the other to achieve completion, depicting the floating world, the art of living in the moment.

There were huge demonstrations in 1969 and 1970 against the US incursion into Cambodia, and I watched from inside the gates of the US embassy as massive flood-lit crowds surged forward in a huge 's' curve, executing the 'snake dance' that was strictly forbidden for reasons that eluded me and which were never fully explained.

They chanted in a synchronised chorus, '*Amerika ka Cambodia!*' – 'America, get out of Cambodia!' Police waited around the corner with shields and batons, like blue soldier crabs waiting for the turn of the tide.

Given a hard white helmet by one of the student demonstrators, my son proudly wore it everywhere, not understanding that the kanji symbols on the side meant 'America, go home!' One day a taxi driver asked us the usual question: '*Amerikajin desuka?*' 'Are you American?' I replied, *'Tie chigaimasu* (No, it's different). *Australiajin desu.*' And he promptly launched into a stirring rendition of – as he sang it – 'God save our Queen, Gracious!', at which my son and I wept with laughter. He was not surprised. We were *gaijin*; therefore, anything was to be expected of us.

Eve had completely lost patience with me. She did not appreciate Japan, its traditional cherry blossom festivals, nor the collective rapture over brightly coloured *momiji* leaves that turn from bright yellow to deep crimson in autumn. Why live in a foreign land as a struggling single mother, and not come home to wattle, grevillea and gum blossom? She waged a relentless campaign for me to return to Australia, so she could ensure I did not take lovers and become like Jean. But I would not give in and did not return until residency was required for me to secure a divorce. I felt that neither Eve nor Bob could begin to understand me, or why I lived in Japan. But it was only by living there and not in the comfort of my homeland that I had come to see that I would never fully comprehend my parents or in return be understood by them, and I accepted that. Unfair perhaps to Bob and Eve, but I was young and obstinate. I needed to forge a path for myself completely separate from them.

1968

I was painting in my tiny studio in Seoul, surrounded by deep banks of snow, at Christmas when I saw our cousin Tony die. It was a savage winter in Korea, armed guards at the pedestrian crossings, curfews, and an unending strain of the Cold War confrontation with the north. A window suddenly slid open in my head, and in that window, Tony died. I slammed it shut, terrified of this omen of second sight. Two weeks later, my husband handed me a thin blue airmail letter, slit open at the edges. He had not made the mistake he made a month earlier when he handed me an unopened letter, which was written in a woman's hand and began, *My darling*. It was from his lover. I handed that letter back, saying, 'I believe this is yours.' Now, I was holding this second letter, begging him to tell me who it was about, who had died. But he would not speak and opening it I read that Tony was dead, his helicopter down in flames, 3 January 1969, in Vietnam. His death exploded inside me, a crater that never healed. I didn't want it to heal, wanted the knowledge of Tony to go on aching forever. Soon after I had read both blue airmail letters, my husband and I began the process of divorce.

Tony and I had said goodbye in January 1968, after having coffee together near David Jones, both going overseas and feeling sophisticated and adult. I kissed him farewell, a young married woman with a small son, and never again in such command of my universe. When I glanced back, Tony was leaning against the wall, watching me walk away, and the look on his face bruised my heart. I had forgotten he was headed to war.

Tony came home in a blue aluminium military coffin draped with a flag. The coffin could not be opened because there were too many separate pieces of Tony for his mother to view. Or that's what they claimed. Sub. Lieutenant Anthony Jeffrey Huelin, death date 3 January 1969, UNIT RAN Helicopter Flight Vietnam, Service – 9th October 1968 – 3 January 1969; a total of 117 days and four months. Four used to be my lucky number. It is the number for death in Japan. The night before I married, I found a bottle of Je Reviens perfume under my pillow, a round deep-blue glass flask. It was from Tony. 'Je Reviens' means 'I will return.' But he didn't.

*　　　　*　　　　*　　　　*

Tony lay with a mouth full of mud that oozed lazily between his teeth, under his tongue, the silky earth pulverised by centuries of rain, the reflux of river deltas and decayed jungle. It tasted like salty chocolate, bitter with blood. It tasted like tadpoles and slime. Tadpoles now swam from Tony's mouth up into his brain, poking easily past the nasal bone, penetrating the cranium to burst whole and lively into the spinning cavity that was his head. They swam faster and faster, until all that was left was the blur of their black-green movement, the strange, acrid, primeval taste.

Far above Tony, helicopters buzzed like maddened mosquitos in air dense with smoke and shells. Bombs erupted with monotonous hiccups in the jungle, erasing a village here and there, shredding lives, idly dismembering arms, and legs, voiding shrapnel into the acid haze. The countryside sweated rot and fumes. Vast green leaves rode tattered umbrellas over enemy and friend, living and dead alike. The chirr of insects, the seeping jungle and muddy deltas converged into an enveloping liquidity.

Shallow sensations lapped at Tony, filmy waves of pain crimping up then ebbing away. Moments passed where nothing happened but a slight rise and fall of breath. Then a stronger surge would wash up over the one before, swirling depth over depth until a cobalt tunnel sucked him in, rolled over and swept him out.

Undertow is the following force of a wave, its unexpected subtraction. Offshore waves roll in serried ranks like decorous schoolchildren clad in indigo. Then the magnetic pull of the land forces the pace; they break rank, cresting in white spume and spitting soapy froth, crash copycat, one over the other to extinguish in a milk moustache traced in sand. Mute and fierce, the water sucks itself back, absent one minute, the next an urgent slurry that forces the swimmer back out and under, until nothing is left but the spinning molecules that make up blueness.

*   *   *   *

I shut my teeth against Tony's death. Seeing it written so plainly on a blue airmail letter squeezed all the oxygen from my heart. That happy, wild boy, part of my life for so many years, had disintegrated. His laughter, his grin and teasing jokes, his curly hair was gone, and my shocked spirit attempted to act as if not mortally wounded. 'Where to now?' I asked my husband after receiving the news of Tony's death and accompanied him dry-eyed to a tailor where he was being fitted for a new overcoat. A Korean friend walking in downtown Seoul saw my face through the window, came in and took me away to sit with her. She fed me small pieces of steak, determined that I would eat, and asked me questions; she was the only one I ever talked to about Tony. 'You have to leave,' she told me. I hardly needed her encouragement. Meanwhile, the endless parties among the diplomats continued, sometimes so drunkenly that one man fell into my unlit fireplace after throwing his heart at my unwelcoming feet. I was in despair.

At one of the parties, the French ambassador's wife, who had a soft spot for me, said, 'You are an artist, and when you leave here you will go to Paris!' But I didn't want Paris and the world of the Impressionists and surrealism. 'No,' I replied, 'I want to go to New York.' In 1967, before leaving for Korea, I had seen an exhibition of new American painting, 'Two Decades of American Painting in Australia', at the Art Gallery of New South Wales. It was rich with works by Jackson Pollock, Jasper Johns, Andy Warhol, Ad Reinhardt, Barnett Newman, Helen Frankenthaler and Cy Twombly. It seemed large-spirited, ambitious and open-hearted, despite the political baggage of the Cold War, Vietnam and anti-American sentiment. To me, it looked like the future. If New York was where contemporary art was happening, then one day I would go there. But at that party, talking to the French ambassador's wife, I had no plan for New York. I had to undo my marriage first.

*   *   *   *

I travelled home after Korea and Japan, to the land where I was born, the land from which Tony was now gone forever. My mother went to his funeral and held his mother, her sister-in-law Pauline, in her arms, but refused to talk about it. When things hurt so deeply, she kept silent – she always did. After nine months in Australia, enduring cool disapproval for my divorce, I left for America at the end of 1970. My sister and mother saw me off at Sydney airport, better attuned than I to the fact that I was leaving permanently, and went out and bought false eyelashes afterwards. Did it stop them seeing how far I was going?

*   *   *   *

At last, in 1972, I was finally living in New York, where I spent the next forty years of my life, feeling the peculiar, detached belonging so characteristic of the city. The sight of its buildings shoving each other aside to get at the light delighted me, as they vertically strove to best each other. I could walk everywhere, the basic grid of the street pattern suited me, and I rode the subways and went anywhere I could. New York was the centre of the world and behaved like it. To be in New York was to be somewhere, and once a citizen of New York, always a citizen of New York. Manhattan taught a brand of striving, dangled a chance at success, described best in E.B. White's immortal words in *Here Is New York*:

> On any person who desires such queer prizes,
> New York will bestow the gift of loneliness
> and the gift of privacy ... for the residents of
> Manhattan are to a large extent strangers who
> have pulled up stakes somewhere and come to
> town, seeking sanctuary or fulfillment or some
> greater or lesser grail. The capacity to make such
> dubious gifts is a mysterious quality of New York.
> It can destroy an individual, or it can fulfill him,
> depending a good deal on luck. No one should
> come to New York to live unless he is willing to
> be lucky.

New York was the centre of the contemporary art world then – male, misogynistic and discriminatory, it was dominated by the famous art critic Clement Greenberg, who told me when I refused to sleep with him, 'You don't know how to behave!' During alcohol- and drug-infused loft parties in Soho, surrounded by paintings in progress and the rags of artistic poverty, I sat carefully propped against a wall, watching, never participating. One night the famous painter Helen Frankenthaler, eyeing me coldly, removed her gloves slowly and deliberately, finger by finger, then shook my hand and left. Philosophical and brilliant Robert Motherwell was kind, and Kenneth Noland, full of high spirits, advised me, 'Let a painting breathe.' Stewart Waltzer was the funniest artist and friend I had ever met, even though to him I was a hopeless case 'from somewhere else, not even from New York!' Anne Truitt, the brave and intelligent colour-field minimalist sculptor ('minimalist' being a category, she told me, she didn't think defined her work), became a dear friend and advised that I audit classes at the Institute of Fine Arts. The art history I learned, the museums and galleries, the hungry artists theorising and experimenting, all opened my eyes to what might be possible, even for one as intransigent as me. I was prepared to accept all of it, good luck, or none at all, whatever came my way, because I was in New York, I was working, and I belonged.

IV

During the years my parents still lived at the farm, I had travelled home once again from New York and Eve was driving me there up over the Blue Mountains from Sydney. We stopped beside the road and got out to look over the edge at the view from the cliffs, sheared off long ago by block escarpment. It was a bright day, and the honey-coloured sandstone resembled the inside of Violet Crumble bars; the air was mauve, blue bush scented with gum leaves, a trickle of water curdling secretively on the valley floor below. I remembered being told as a child that if I got caught in a bushfire I should run downhill and find water to lie in. Banksia were flowering, and a circle of buzzing flies nearby slowly came into focus. I peered down and saw, half-hidden by low scrub, the pale carcass of a huge dog, a Great Dane, completely flayed. It looked raw, pinkly indecent. Menace bloomed abruptly from the swirl of avid flies and the inert creature at the edge of the bush. We hurried to the car and drove away. Years later, I asked Eve if she remembered this, and she claimed I had made it up. 'You have a very good memory, Judith,'

she said jeeringly, using the tone she always took if she
didn't want to admit something.

*   *   *   *

'O, call back yesterday, bid time return,' Shakespeare
wrote in *Richard II*, and so it would be, looking back
from so far away in New York, remembering postwar
life in Oberon in 1946. The countryside then felt bleak,
still riven with privation, sons, fathers, uncles, brothers,
and cousins missing, the community and whole country
mourning all its lost men. There was a sense of something
dangerous and improbable always lurking, like the flayed
dog I had discovered with such horror at the edge of the
bush. We were all wary. It was so difficult to understand
that the war had ended, even for a child. I remember
sitting through a memorial service on my uncle Monty's
knee, Tony next to us. Monty winced when I wriggled.
I had forgotten he had been shot during the war for
which they were now playing the 'Last Post' in homage
and remembrance. He was my father's younger brother,
a hero ace pilot who flew throughout the war, from the
Battle of Britain through to the Burma campaign. He was
shot down in Burma, a bullet passing through his knee
breaking the bones. Somehow, he managed to fly back
to base, the only one of his unit to survive. Now back in

Oberon, it was Monty who was most often the centre of fun. He had bought a small de Havilland Tiger Moth plane, which he kept in the Oberon's bus shed. When he took it out to fly on weekends, the whole town turned out, captivated when he took off or landed, and overcome with hilarity when he misjudged his landing site and tore through a farmer's barbed-wire fence instead.

Once he took me up in the plane with him. I wore a little leather helmet and put my head out the side, opening my mouth wide so the air could rush in and blow up my cheeks like a balloon. We zoomed over paddocks, houses and sheep from high in the air. Magic. Coming back with him from a family picnic, I explained to him that I had never gone over forty miles an hour in a car, and soon we were racing in his little grey Citroen at what felt like at least one hundred miles an hour but was probably sixty. He tried to teach me how to turn my eyelids inside out, but I never quite mastered the trick. When he drove us to Parkes to catch the train to our grandparents in Broken Hill for holidays, we played I-Spy. When I chose 'something beginning with m', he roared with delight that it was his moustache. He worked with my father and his brother John at the sawmill, which became – and still – is a major employer in the Oberon area.

Family picnics in the bush with aunts, uncles and cousins were a constant, with campfires, roasted sausages and chops, tea boiled black and sweet in billycans, and wading in trout streams like the Duckmaloi with utter delight, because water was still rare and there was no town pool or lake to swim in. Later, a small concrete pool was built, but it was so ignored that it finally yielded to slime and tadpoles. One summer, the church organised for a bus-load of families to travel to a large public swimming pool at Blackheath, lower down the Blue Mountains. It was a wonderful day, hot and sunny, sandwiches, swimsuits, raspberry cordial, splashing, diving, everyone having fun. The adults were happy and laughing, too, when suddenly the whole place went quiet. One of the larger boys, about eight years old, had put a smaller one who wanted to see the deep end onto his shoulders, giving him a ride. As he kept walking, nobody understood that he was drowning, stalled under the deep water at the end of the pool. A dreadful silence swept over us. Families were packed up and rushed back to the bus. What happened to his mother and father? What happened to the little boy on his shoulders? Eve refused to say. The subject was not open. It is too late now, as it was too late then. Joy comes with teeth.

1949

After the difficult business of trying to understand this cold country backwater where she now lived with three small children, Eve decided she would raise stud sheep. She opted for Hampshire Downs, the best-looking breed, and for just that reason. She began with George and Cheeky, two rams who came to live in our backyard while we still lived in the little town of Oberon. Tony, Rob and I liked to tease George and Cheeky by pushing down on their foreheads till they lowered their heads and charged. Squealing gleefully, we would race across the grass and up a ladder propped against the clothesline, just out of their reach, which further infuriated them. They would try to climb the steps with their hooves and seemed to love the chase as much as we did, waiting by the back gate for us to come home from school.

*   *   *   *

Before we moved to the farm, my brother and I discovered an Irish drunk named Bricky, deeply hidden in the bush on a hilltop behind our house. He lived there in a small canvas tent, and we would take our afternoon tea of raspberry cordial and Iced Vo-Vo biscuits to keep him company beside his small campfire, while he got shickered. He taught us how to use his small axe to cut thin eucalypt saplings and bend and weave them into crude shelters patterned after Aboriginal humpies. This relationship continued in a friendly way until he took a ticket in the Red Cross town lottery as a surprise for me. It was the only time I ever won anything – a large china doll with blue glass eyes that opened and shut. I hated it. Eve finally learned about Bricky when I was handed the prize in Mawhood's grocery store, where she was shopping. The locals writhed with bemused delight as Eve grasped my upper arm and squeezed it ferociously, saying through tightly clenched teeth behind her scarlet lipstick, 'Say thank you to Mr Bricky, dear!' It was the type of arm squeeze that lets you know you are in the deepest kind of shit. We never saw Bricky again. The locals were amused by her setback and my wildness. Australians love a good come down for anyone on the rise like Bob and Eve. As the Japanese proverb puts it, *'Deru kugi wa utareru,'* or 'The nail that protrudes will be hammered down.'

When we moved from the desert to the western slopes of the Blue Mountains, we discovered a cold high country with frost, snow and disapproving people. We were strangers and they weren't, so everything we did was suspect. My father was elected to the Oberon Shire Council and argued for a bitumen road to replace the old dirt road from Bathurst. The locals didn't like it one bit. 'We don't want all sorts of strange people coming here to Oberon,' they declared.

*　　　*　　　*　　　*

Walking in the deep bush at the back farm with my father, I was chattering away like a parrot when he grabbed my shoulder to silence me. Standing right beside us, as tall as my father and equally composed, was a huge old male red kangaroo. We stood for what seemed an eternity, looking into his eyes, until slowly he moved away. What did he tell us through those eyes? Tales of long ago, of Aboriginal people, the original people, and a time when this stolen land was theirs and his, no thieving white people from a green and rainy island shooting and killing. We did not realise we were them.

*　　　*　　　*　　　*

My desert-born parents had become farmers and under-stood the fundamentals of a steady water supply. Relying on rain in that country was tantamount to believing in unicorns. Rain was almost a hallucination, a fragrant smell that meant nothing, a mirage that did not bleed water. Eve hired a water diviner, and a white-haired man arrived at the farm with a long, thin, right-angled iron rod and a huge willow branch shaped like a tuning fork. With the angled rod, he walked away from where he claimed lines of water ran deep under the land. He strode with impressive confidence from these invisible streams, and the rod in his hand turned back towards them. We watched in awe, but my father was amused. He did not believe in water divining; he was humouring Eve. The diviner held out the rod to me and told me to walk away from the underground stream I could not see. I walked away, and almost to my horror the rod turned uncannily in my hand, pointing back to where he said the water ran. Then he picked up the willow fork and held its two pronged branches, shaped like chicken wishbones, upright over the point he claimed lines of water converged. Despite his locked grip, the force of underground water pulled the fork down so hard that a branch the circumference of my ten-year-old wrist snapped. An artesian bore was sunk, which yielded 500 gallons a minute. It never failed, and no matter how harsh the season, our crops were watered. Long aluminium sprinklers spouted a gentle mineral rain into the dry air, arcing rainbows down onto turnips, corn, peas, potatoes, and hay. We would sit on the soft earth after the potatoes had been dug, sieving for tiny fingerlings left behind, or eat peas fresh from vines so sweet it felt as if green had burst in our mouths. Eve had us shell huge hessian bags of fresh picked peas, which she then steamed and stacked in the large hall freezer. Later, she would entertain with elaborate dinners, cooking gourmet meals featuring her speciality, duck a l'Orange, abetted by those peas. By then my father had entered politics, and important guests had begun to visit.

*   *   *   *

Eve got her stud sheep to breed in 1956, and when her run as a stud breeder ended in 1981, she had grown one of the best and biggest Hampshire Down studs in the southern hemisphere. One winter night, a huge trailer truck brought the first of the pregnant ewes to the farm. Attempting to negotiate the poplar trees that lined the drive before turning into the front paddock, the truck stuck fast in mud. Light snow whipped the air. A barricade of hay bales had been stacked as shelter for the ewes, and the farm manager bustled about organising their unloading. Nervous and unsteady, the ewes walked down the truck's ramp into the cold. They were a mysterious grey-white colour with black ears, eyes, and legs. We were wild with excitement, especially Eve, anxious for her new charges in the extreme cold. These sheep were her new overtures and concertos, and they grew to love her. The farm manager raddled the bellies of the rams

SWIMMING HOME

with blue or red chalk, and when they were put in with
the ewes that were ready to breed, Eve would know which
sire had mounted which ewe, indicating the bloodlines of
the resulting lamb. She kept exquisite stud books with
bloodlines inked like lines of music. She was writing her
own variation of 'Sheep May Safely Graze', the Bach aria
she would instruct us to play at her funeral.

The sheep pen was moved near the house, and one
cold morning we found the newborn lambs ailing, their
tongues blue. Australia had harsh import restrictions as
a guard against livestock disease, especially bluetongue
and scrapie, but we feared that the disease had somehow breached the barriers. The vet was sent for, and
we waited for the dreaded diagnosis, which would have
meant all livestock on the farm, including my dog, Lisa,
would have to be destroyed. My mother was pale with
anxiety, and I wanted to vomit, but it turned out that
the lambs had pneumonia, not bluetongue. Eve fed them
an enriched formula of raw eggs, cream and brandy, the
same thing we fed her in 1960, presuming that what had
worked for the lambs would work with her too as she lay
in an oxygen tent in St Luke's Hospital in Sydney, danger-
ously ill with double pneumonia.

*　　　*　　　*　　　*

Eve spent hours with her studbooks – her handwriting, notations and columns as neat as musical scores, dams and sires and their progeny marked like clefs and quavers. The sheep were her project. She was no longer restricted to a wounded duckling in a pocket or a lame dog. It was serious business now. Striving for perfection, she would sometimes breed ewes past their prime. One old ewe nicknamed 'Hoppy' had a uterus that everted after a birth. The prolapse was tied back and held in place with a large beer bottle. This didn't work, and Eve came down the hill from the barn in tears and sent me to gather pills from the medicine cabinet to mix a lethal potion. In the small paddock, we sat together with Hoppy's head in our laps as Eve fed her the mixture, weeping as the old ewe slowly died.

*　　　　*　　　　*　　　　*

I was angry with Eve. I thought stud breeding unfair to animals. But the ewes loved her, and she would go down to the fenced paddock below the house in the late afternoons and call out, 'Come on, my girls! Come on, my dears!' and they would stream across the paddock to eat bread from her hands as she scratched their pointy black ears that smelt of lanolin and grass. When they lambed, Eve stayed in the sheds with them late into the night, slipping her small pianist's hands up birth canals to turn long-legged lambs stuck crosswise in maiden ewes and slide out slippery bundles of new life. She would return to the house at midnight, hands swollen from the birth struggle, clothing covered in mucus and blood, her spirit radiant. At last, the pianist had her pastoral symphony.

I hated the 'miracle of birth' that Eve kept going on about, appalled to learn it would be part of my future. When she asked if I wanted to learn about menstruation and sex, I refused to listen. So, she didn't tell me, and I had almost no idea of what was involved in menstruation, sexual intercourse or protection until I became pregnant and gave birth myself. Eve probably thought that my ignorance would 'serve me right' for not listening to her. 'What did you do?' she would ask when I came home from a party, but I was careful to omit anything of the slightest interest, only relating details about food or clothing, keeping my world secret from her. But Eve was too busy to care. She was busy because Bob was busy. Bob intended to rise, and rise he did.

1949

Joining the Liberal Party as a young man, Bob was asked to run against the deeply popular Labor prime minister Ben Chifley in the seat of Macquarie in 1949. 'You won't win,' he was told, 'but run so hard you force him back to campaign in his home district', taking his attention away from the federal campaign. Everywhere we went we pasted stickers onto step risers that said, *Watch your step! Vote Cotton!* Eve and Bob ran so hard that although they lost – and Chifley was succeeded as prime minister by the Liberal Party's Robert Menzies – Bob drew Chifley's interest, and after the election he asked him to consider joining the Labor Party. A centrist by nature, Bob deliberated hard but decided against it, as he didn't agree with Labor's policy of nationalising the banks. But they stayed friendly, and when Chifley was dying of cancer, Bob was one of the few asked to visit him. We walked in Chifley's funeral parade in 1951 in Bathurst, with Eve carrying a thermos of hot pea soup for us. 'Why is that man wearing a towel on his head?' I asked her about the Indian dignitary marching in front of us, never having seen a turban before.

1956

'We have to kill the fox!' Eve declared. It was slipping into the lambing paddock, the long paddock at the farm, boldly russet and visible in daylight, and biting the noses off lambs being born. It killed for pleasure, tearing the heads off twenty of Eve's Muscovy ducks one night because it could, not bothering to eat them. Eve wanted that fox gone, and my brother and I, determined and passionate marksmen, tried to help by shooting at it with the .22 rifle. We missed every time, the fox outsmarting us. Eve decided to lay a trap for the cunning murderer. 'Go out and shoot me a bird,' she said to my brother and me. As we walked up the hill towards the barns, I saw a bird move in a tree, raised the gun, and shot. The bird fell to earth. 'You shot it, you pick it up,' my brother said. When I did, I found to my stomach-roiling horror that it was a parrot. I had shot that which I loved when I aimed to kill. Eve did not waste the bird, though, putting poisoned wheat in its bill and laying it in the fox's path. The fox ate the bird, and for that season the lambs survived, while I ate the savage lesson of regret.

The local farmers organised a fox shoot. Not part of the native fauna, the foxes had been brought by homesick English immigrants to Australia, where, with no regional predators, they grew much larger. My sister and I were instructed to be beaters, silently walking five feet apart through the bush as part of the drive to force the foxes towards the line of shooters. It wasn't called Shooters Hill for nothing. Chatting idly, we strolled lackadaisically through the trees. My brother was enraged when we reached the shooters at last. 'Sit here and shut up!' he demanded, putting us on a fallen tree with the .410 shotgun he thought I would cause little damage with. He was not wrong. As my sister and I sat chatting again, I saw the fox heading towards us through the bush. The gun was cocked open. I clicked it closed and fired. The barrel jammed. In a panic I tried to load the other barrel but failed, and the fox walked past me, apparently sniggering. 'Get in the ute and go home,' my brother told us, disgusted.

Later, I had another meeting with a fox when my lover Yale took me to see the start of an impeccably tailored fox hunt in the lush, rolling green hills of WASPy Dutchess County in New York State. He had grown up riding as a passionately integral part of these Anglophilic fox hunts. I started to laugh. 'Don't you know you live in America?' I said, and he had a similar reaction to my brother: 'Get in the car and go home!'

*   *   *   *

Walking up the hill to the house from the trees near the dam, Bob carried a tiny pink embryo, a hatchling kookaburra having fallen from its nest, barely alive. Eve took the bird from him, made a nest of cottonwool for it and using tweezers fed it breadcrumbs soaked in milk. Unexpectedly, the bird lived, graduating to worms she had dug and chopped up for it, and growing into a fully-fledged male we called Sid. Sid flew about his home in our kitchen, trying to produce the full-throated cackle of his peers. He could manage the first part – 'hoo-hoo-hoo' – but failed to grasp the falling cadence that slipped into 'ha-ha-ha', so we would accompany his chortles, attempting to teach him the musical run up that spilt into complete avian laughter. Released into the garden, Sid lived there for months before mating and nesting in a nearby grove of stringybark trees. When Eve walked out into the garden to hang laundry to dry, Sid would swoop down from his roost and perch on her shoulder. Eve, the bird whisperer.

I never agreed with any of Eve's aesthetic choices. When she asked how I wanted my room at the farm to be decorated, I said, 'White with checked curtains.' I returned from boarding school to a deep-pink room, bed heavily flounced and quilted in blue roses on a white background, with matching curtains, rose light fixtures and

a bedside lamp studded with plaster flowers. My mother
and I were as mismatched as the room to my personality.

About this time, when I was fifteen and wanting to be an
artist, I read that Cezanne carried a copy of Baudelaire's
'*Une Charogne*' ('A Carcass') in his pocket. Misunder-
standing the poem's misogyny, I thought it implied an
artist must be able to look at anything and find beauty
in it. I went down to the front paddock one hot summer
afternoon with my drawing book and pencil and sat down
in front of a dead sheep. It had been rotting for some
days, and maggots were crawling through its tangled
shards of fleece and flesh. I lasted five minutes inspecting
the swollen corpse under its hum of feasting flies.

*   *   *   *

My sister had a strong right arm, which she would use
in adulthood for a successful career as a sculptor carving
marble, stone and wood. As many sisters do, we could
rub each other raw. When she used that strong arm to
pummel me, I would scratch her as hard as I could. 'How
did you get that scratch?' Eve would ask her. 'I walked
into a barbed-wire fence,' she would answer stoically.
My brother tried to arbitrate but it was no use. She was
older, I was younger, so I was going to challenge her every

power play. When boys first began to telephone her, I was merciless, hiding behind the couch then leaping about and crowing while she tried to exchange halting pleasantries with them. How could she develop into a young woman, get engaged and settle with apparent complacency into wedlock? I watched as she was solemnly robed in a heavy satin embroidered wedding gown like some Spanish grandee's daughter, poised to enter a land I could not understand. I gulped with something very like fright when the veil was put over her head. I will not do that, I thought, and chose serial monogamy instead, not the long road taken. Did this make me the wicked Jean to her steadfast Eve?

1957

I left our second boarding school, Marsden, at sixteen, finishing school a grade early. Eve tried to talk me into returning for another year, to stay out of her way, but I refused – eight years away was too much. For my seventeenth birthday, Eve allowed me to have a puppy named Lisa, but she insisted I was the one who must decide whether to spay or breed her. I had a nightmare that I chose to spay her, and the vet slashed a deep cross down her face that caused her eyeballs to fly out. I chose to spay her anyway. I could not forget the sight of the small breeding females in the kennel, who had learnt to climb the chain-link fence by clinging on with desperate claws, attempting escape.

After Lisa was spayed, I went to bed and thought about my future. Eve and Bob's need for staff as their political lives expanded had grown exponentially, sweeping everyone and everything into their service. Considering this, I felt that I had three choices: stay and go under as a staff aide; break with them completely but stay intact; or leave and still be able to love them. Like the small dogs in the kennel, I knew I must escape, leave my home and family and country, leave Lisa and all I loved behind. Years after I was gone Lisa died from snakebite, and Eve, who had cared for her, would never have a dog again. When her two white cats – with gentian violet painted on their ears to prevent skin cancer – died, she would not have another cat either. It had become unsafe for her to love. Years later, I found a black-and-white photograph of two dogs. Written on the back were the names Mickey and Paddy. I knew about Mickey, the dog she loved, but these were Irish names she had given them, and I knew Eve detested the Irish. She was very proud of her Scottish blood, which she inherited from Archie Macdougall. But later she discovered she had Irish blood too. Bloodlines, like musical scores, are a tricky business.

*   *   *   *

Next door to Eve at the house in Oberon on Jenolan Street, a piano was endlessly ravaging the 'Rach 3', Rachmaninoff's *Piano Concerto No. 3*, which had riveted the world in 1958 when Harvey Lavan 'Van' Cliburn won the first quadrennial International Tchaikovsky Piano Competition in Moscow, blowing away the Cold War competition. Now Marie, the girl who lived next door to Eve, ceaselessly practised the 'Rach 3'. 'Not good enough,' her mother said to Marie, and told my mother so. Listening with an ear exquisitely attuned for tone, Eve shuddered for Marie. 'Not the slightest chance she will ever, ever be good enough.' The practising went on all year, and all the next, repeating endlessly, until one day there was sudden silence. Standing on a chair behind the door, Marie killed her father – the local chemist, Mr Osborne – and her endlessly disapproving mother. How did she do it? Hiding behind the door, she must have used some heavy instrument, maybe an axe, maybe a hammer, or a frying pan. Where was her mother when Marie killed him? Did she see the murder and scream, so Marie was forced to kill her too? Or was she going to kill her anyway? 'Mahhrrree' was how the Osbornes pronounced the name of their only child. After the trial verdict of insanity – because only an insane woman would kill her parents – Marie was put away at the discretion of the governor. The insanity plea meant that should she ever appear sane, and an application be filed for her release, the governor could decide to keep her imprisoned. I did not learn any of this until I was in my late thirties and living in New York.

By then my mother no longer found it necessary to hide this information from me. In 1978 my father, retired from politics, was now representing his country in my adopted city. Eve wore a mink coat and was the wife of Australia's consul general. She was Lady Cotton now, had lunched with the Queen, and watched her husband kneel in Buckingham Palace as the Queen tapped him on each shoulder with her sword. He stood up as Sir Robert, Knight of the Order of St Michael and St George, wearing morning dress. My son and I, watching from the balcony, decided independently of each other to steal hand towels from the palace bathrooms, but they only supplied paper, apparently accustomed to Australians. Eve had arrived, not on the pianist's path she had once chosen, or as a brilliant stud sheep breeder, but as the wife of that very successful man from Broken Hill who had the will and yeast for rising. He led, it was true, but she could often mentally clear-cut the path instead, being sharper and more discerning about people than my father, who was still rather open-hearted in a way that her heart was only ever open to animals.

Eve thought about the murdered chemist who had once opened oysters at our parties, thought about their small, stolid brick house with a red tiled roof, windows cramped tight with cream paint, and a small front garden that marched pansies down each side of a cement path. The Osborne house stood between our white house with blue trim and our grandparents' house, used mostly during Christmas holidays. The whole family gathered there for the Christmas night pantomime our parents wrote and acted, singing and dancing and wearing mops on their heads as wigs while we cousins rolled on the floor, laughing. On the long drive to Oberon from Broken Hill, in his black Studebaker with the folding jump seats we loved, Grandfather Leslie almost always hit a kangaroo. It was a long way home for him and my grandmother Muriel, and kangaroos owned the road.

Eve took out her good woollen suit, with the fitted jacket and pencil skirt, tailored for her in London during the six-month world trip that all good colonials on the rise made in those days. When the tailor on Bond Street placed the tape around Eve's upper arm, taking her measurements, he drew back in supercilious disapproval, saying, 'Oh, madam! Surely not scrubbing?' She was abashed but remained unafraid of scrubbing. She lifted her head high at the memory and put on the black hat with a swoop of green feathers that curved around her ear, then screwed small pearl earrings onto her earlobes. She pulled on black kid gloves and drove to the funeral for the murdered local chemist and his wife. Maybe she went as much in sympathy for Marie and her inadequate rendition of the 'Rach 3'.

When we lived in Oberon town we had a black Wolseley sedan, with running boards that swooped up and over the front tyres. When we washed it, we would slide down the soap bubbles on the running boards and fall off their ends. But now that we lived at the farm, we had a large dark blue Daimler with a chestnut dashboard. Eve had it cleaned by workers at the farm, rubbed with a damp chamois till it shone, and then she drove it to the church. She turned down the farm's driveway, lined with poplars my father thought looked like those in France, and headed to town four miles away. As she turned her head in her red-rimmed glasses, the hat feathers tickled her neck. She was a good driver, a brilliant cook, an imaginative and daring gardener, far better than Ollie with her blue hydrangeas and toadflax (Linaria). Whatever Eve planted flourished: roses, peonies, mock orange, cumquats, strawberries, raspberries and cherries. Whatever she cooked was as perfect as a musical score. She never spoke about the funeral or told us about the murder until years later in New York. There was so much she never said.

*   *   *   *

In 1959 the barns that housed the stud sheep caught fire. It was spontaneous combustion from the hay stacked inside. The locals drove up our driveway and parked, not about to miss the close view of a fire raging on someone else's property, especially someone as high profile as Bob. Five of Eve's prize rams were penned inside the barn. Terrified of the flames, they stayed mute and were burnt alive. Eve, whose spirit must have been in a state of dreadful damage, insisted I dress right then, as the flames immolated the barn, in my best suit and go to the local church to serve as godmother to my youngest cousin. I walked to the font with my eyes watery from smoke, and later, against my will, obeyed Eve's demand that I return to Sydney University instead of staying to help as any family member would with a burning barn and dead sheep. How she must have wept privately.

V

1979

I had just returned to the house in Balmoral when the wallaby died. The day before, I had watched my sister walk through the lowering beauty of the light to feed her, as if it were an ordinary thing to do. It was. Stumbling out of bed with jet lag the next morning, I heard a small struggle in the bush below, and looking over the verandah saw the wallaby lying among the tree ferns, head flung back in a rictus that had it almost meet the sturdy whip of tail that was her counterpoise. Above the white muzzle, her large dark eyes were blank. A small trickle of blood ran from her right ear.

This was the dark undertow of home. Wildness extinguished in a suburban garden, the heartsick dichotomy that faces the returning expatriate, dazzled with the land's savage beauty, each memory a stroke of the lash marking that soon it will be gone. 'You could never live here now,' my sister declared. 'They wouldn't let you.' Who were *They*? My presence seemed to stir up troubling antagonisms, as if I were some unruly, sea beast disturbing the blue waters locked around this drowsy island. 'Go back where you came from!' seemed to be implied. But this was where I came from.

And yet the child in me does not doubt that I can return to seas that slide in a silver sheet on long empty beaches as if erasing the notion of human existence – return to melting ice cream, bare feet running in bush paddocks, parrots, snakes, bushfires, and trees that seem as eccentric as close friends; does not doubt that miles and square miles of freedom are mine. But that is the child in me. Australia is still my inner landscape that lets me in and shuts me out, so that returning to America I feel as if I've jammed the fingers of my emotions in a door.

*   *   *   *

Now, looking out to where the ancient chalky paws of the Heads sprawled sphinx-like, relishing their grip on the Pacific, I was transfixed by the sight of a lone bather on the rocks below, wet towel flapping in the wind. I felt my childhood creep back and slept that night lulled by the sound of waves as the earth turned, rolled itself around the sun and blasted light indoors on its screeching return at dawn. I was bemused by the unexpected speckling inside the beaks of the kookaburras reaching for meat on the verandah railing, by the lorikeets begging for food from the feathery mass of khaki, red-tipped bush, wary with the memory that funnel-web, trapdoor and red-back spiders signalled that Australia that can be deadly, hiding poison in small, quiet unexpected packages, sea wasps, blue-ringed octopi, box jellyfish, snakes.

The death of the wallaby evoked the memory of pregnant ewes at the farm, stranded on their sides heavy with twins, unable to protect themselves against the crows who would seize the opportunity to peck their eyes out. It is called a 'murder of crows' for a reason. These ewes gave birth like a struggling Oedipus, antiseptic powder puffed into their ruined, bloody sockets. It also brought back the choking smell of bushfires, the fly-blown maggots that ruined farmers' lives, torn between drought, fire and flood, a harsh land for those from another hemisphere attempting to turn it green.

*   *   *   *

'Aah! Aah! Aaah!' I heard the pecking crows in my mind as I took the bus to Wynyard, reliving time past as I walked along George Street, Martin Place, and turned onto Macquarie Street by the Mitchell Library, across from the Botanical Gardens. I remembered my university years when the books I was supposed to study for exams would all be checked out from there by serious students when I finally arrived. In those days I would straggle away empty-handed, towards the Domain, past the palm trees, idly feeling their bumps with my fingers, wondering how to bluff my way through one more exam, already guilty at the grade I would get. The palms feel the same now, just taller, and thicker in the waist, well-kept manicured matrons.

I rode back over the harbour, passing ferries named for governors' ladies: the *Lady Cutler, Lady McKell, Lady Woodward, Lady Wakehurst*, all those formidable ladies doing daily penance in their next lives, ferrying workers as busily as they once traversed the starched borders of their social world. 'So sorry! Can't wait! Must get on!' The mad, gaudy smile of Luna Park leered under the bridge, its spiked tiara throbbing with light above the gorgon head. I vaguely remembered shadowy stories of horrible accidents, fires, tortures, teasing gone wrong, a death. But all I really remembered was screaming with glee slithering down its long wooden slides.

As the ferry belched and sidled into Kirribilli wharf, I was eighteen again, imagining myself in love, wearing a tight skirt with new pigskin high heels. One shoe fell into the churning water as I left the ferry, and the man who would become my first husband fished it out of the bobbing wake. 'You'd better come and hold the other one in my pool, so it will be the same colour,' a young woman declared dispassionately, looking at my wet shoe, and led us through her long, terraced garden down to the harbour pool, where we solemnly dunked the other so that the pair would match.

Swimming at Balmoral the next day, I watched children shriek and splash, bare-breasted women floating their nipples with ease in the light surf and saw old brown lizard people walk carefully on the firm patch of sand between wet and dry. A small boy clutched his naked penis and waggled it delightedly in the water. 'That's enough, Adam!' his mother yelled at him. It seemed apt.

*   *   *   *

I returned like a yo-yo again and again from my life on the other side of the world, this time to visit Palm Beach where Bob and Eve now lived. Driving to see them, I was teased by the sense memory of Frenchs Forest that still seems to smell like tossed salad, the lethargic bush split here and there by shards of blackened stumps. At Narrabeen, trees were smothered in pillars of morning glory, an ultramarine weed that choked them with its colourful

grip. In the native palm and casuarinas, cicadas ceaselessly muttered, 'Gum nuts, gum nuts.' A dog barked.

Eve would no longer swim at the beach, not wishing to
be seen even in a cloak of caftan. But sieving my toes
through the particulate crunch of sand I became a shivering kid in a Speedo again, saltwater drying on my skin,
listening for the shark bell, and drinking pineapple juice
through a hole punched in the can. Liquid summer.
I went round the rocks by the pool where the Pacific
hiccupped its briny breath of fish, seaweed, prawns and
shellfish, of sharks and whales sliding under its tossing skin. My feet retained the memory of these rocks,
knew exactly how to climb the bumps and ridges, how
to tiptoe through the scooped pools rimmed with tech-
nicolour anemones. The rocks had been carved by the
sea mimicking its ceaseless smoothing and smothering,
sandstone frozen into a static pattern of repetition, an
eddy, a ripple, a curve of wave, bubbles of foam rendered
negative in rock. I lay on them as day turned into night
and watched the stars wheel overhead in a Van Gogh
sky, feeling the captured heat of the sun irradiate me
while I counted the small light flashes from Barrenjoey
Lighthouse, my father's favourite beacon. Every year we
climbed with him along the dinosaur slump of peninsula
that holds it at arms-length from the beach, sliding back

down the long sandhills to the sea. 1, 2, 3, 4, pause, 1, 2, 3, 4, its light at night acting as a semaphore through time. I am four, seven, twelve, sixteen, twenty-one. I am leaving home. Everything is changing but the light.

I lay beside the carved rock pool where I was taught to swim by Johnny Carter, just one of a generation of summer children, a triangle of white zinc smeared on his nose, hat pulled down low, yelling, 'Blow bubbles!' or 'Keep that melon down!' At six a.m. I would stand at the edge of the pool, wet and shivering till he took pity and released me, then I would jump in the deep end and frolic instead. One day I had just swum twenty-five laps in triumph when Eve ordered me to dive, and I refused. We had a major stand-off and she threatened me with expulsion from the beach and a return to the cloistered boarding house where we were staying. I called her bluff, turned around and headed back to Florida House.

Florida House went on to bigger things, eventually becoming the home of the dominatrix Madame Lash, but in those days it was a boarding house for country families wanting a summer at the beach. It was vital to me then to be deemed equal to or better than the boys, to beat them at their own games, whether boxing, swimming, or terrorising the local adults with a blowpipe cut from bamboo. We stole chicken feed for ammunition – and blew the grain in stinging pellets from a hiding place behind a palm tree. In boxing bouts, I was remorseless, more prepared to hit any boy than they were to hit me. I aimed for their jaws. An older boarder chose me to fetch his morning newspaper, the only girl chosen from among the boys, and with a high heart I ran to the newsagent down between the paperbark trees, twirling nasturtiums that grew beside the road, enchanted by their raw stink. At sixpence a paper I felt I was winning. Outside in the gums the kookaburras hacked and chortled, and the rain-birds whistled and gonged out their passion for the water that fell so rarely from the sky.

We would climb over the headland through the twisted, ghostly angophoras, their elderly bunioned toes clinging to the sandstone strata, silver and lilac sunspots bruising orange skin, and make our way down to Pittwater to chase soldier crabs scuttling in noisy formation along the sand flats and eat cold prawns or hot battered fish and chips wrapped in newspaper from the fish shop. Meanwhile, Eve and Bob would go to the area's famous restaurant, Jonah's, to drink wine and look out over the wide blue Pacific, a paired team harnessed in unison to achieve Bob's dreams.

*   *   *   *

Back in the city, the yachts were tucked away tidily for
the night, the sea so blue and tame it slid past the polished sails of the Opera House like a well-fed crocodile.
The road leads away to Lady Macquarie's Chair, where –
as part of Commemoration Day pranks when university
students could take over the town – one year I helped
shut down traffic, locking lovers in for the evening and
stealing a red traffic lantern for my dorm room. When it
was his turn, my brother sailed in an upside-down beach
umbrella in black tie at night on Sydney Harbour. Now,
Pinchgut Island blinked a single light beside its sole palm,
silver gum leaves turned upside down in a sudden wind
and the aluminium teeth of the yachts chatter together. A
kookaburra chokes and wheezes with laughter as if it had
emphysema, as if it were Bob's father, my grandfather
Leslie, the worrier, dying slowly, lungs struggling for air
as he gasped through green oxygen tanks.

What happened to the old Australia Hotel, with its black
marble face, to tiny Rowe Street and its shop with hand-
made gold bracelets? What happened to polo matches,
to picnic races and balls, to country boys in wide hats
and elastic-sided boots doing their damnedest to grab
a piece of my carefully guarded flesh, braced and boned

into a strapless ballerina ball gown, before taking me home, to long white kid gloves and crushed orchid corsages, long nights of madness when everyone seemed drunk but me?

*   *   *   *

In summer we would make the long drive down the Blue Mountains to the beach north of Sydney, its final headland. One day we woke to discover a cyclone had passed in the night. Bob opened the windows wide, and we watched riveted as the ocean tossed a huge mass of white foam to the horizon, where before it had been carefully combed with cobalt blue waves that broke in white frills on the shore or splashed high up against the sandstone cliffs. That morning Bob took us walking along the shore now strung with sea creatures that had washed up over the road pushed by furious waves into the long gardens of the big houses on the beach. I had never seen an octopus before, a starfish or jellyfish, abandoned like scientific specimens on the dark asphalt, strange underwater creatures lying in pools of foam. It is how I felt when my father died, as if a great wave had gone over me and out to sea, leaving strange jewels of memory, stranded in me like seaweed, asking the questions all children ask about their fathers: *Did I ever really*

*know him? Who was he really? What do I do with the long
empty foreshore now?* He was like the Barrenjoey Lighthouse that he loved, the old fort on the headland at the
end of the beach, transmitting light in intermittent inter-
vals, holding itself apart, able to be reached only through
strenuous effort.

When we would walk with him at night along the beach,
Bob would pick up koalas that had climbed down from
the gum trees and give them to us to hold. Aged nine and
dared by the Morse boys, who were Florida House regu-
lars, I swam out one day well beyond the breakers and felt
glorious with courage, until I realised I was being dragged
out to sea in a riptide. I panicked and started to struggle,
until I saw my father swimming towards me. He could do
anything, it seemed, including saving me.

*   *   *   *

In his maiden speech to parliament when he became
a senator in 1965, with a record one million votes, Bob
quoted the American writer and political commentator
Walter Lippmann:

> The world is a better place to live in because it
> contains human beings who will give up ease and

security and stake their own lives in order to do
what they themselves think worth doing ... They
do the useless, brave, noble, the divinely foolish
and the very wisest things that are done by man.
And what they prove to themselves and to others
is that man is no mere creature of his habits, no
mere automaton in his routine ... but that in the
dust of which he is made there is also fire, lighted
now and then by great winds from the sky.

This metaphor was made for him and the land that
formed him, to which he has now returned as dust. My
last talk with him was on his ninety-first birthday, and he
asked about the US election. 'Who will get up? Where's
the money?' He closed his eyes on Christmas Day in 2006
for the last time. Gough Whitlam had been the prime
minister that Bob, as Senate whip, had helped kick out of
office in 1975 by previously voting to block supply. Later
they became friendly, and when my parents gave Gough
a birthday party one year at their residence in New York,
he studied me carefully and said, 'You have your father's
eyes.' The only time I saw my father's eyes full of tears
was when, weakened with laughter, he would lie his head
down on the table, weeping at a good joke. When he
laughed his whole face would dissolve, eyebrows to the
hairline, hands rubbing his eyes with delight.

'Don't tell your mother!' he told us, having just backed the Land Rover into a tree, and bleeding from a small gash on his forehead. Why would we? We had a pact with this man who sang loudly with us as we drove along Shooters Hill Road to the back farm. 'One man went to mow, went to mow a meadow!' we would shout, then 'Ten green bottles hanging on the wall!' released into wild gaiety by his own. He took absurd delight in fireworks, in fishing in any clear stream for trout, even without much success. Once a plate of rainbow trout, unblemished by any hook, was delivered to him as a gift from locals, who had 'tickled' the trout into highly illegal submission. They would wait until the trout lay somnolent in the shade under the bank of the river, and then stealthily slide their hands into the water to stroke the fish until it relaxed and could be swiftly grabbed. He loved a good burn-off and would have huge stumps bulldozed and cleared in the middle of the paddocks, so that he could set fire to them later risk-free, and we would dance around the flames. Years earlier, as president of the Oberon Shire Council, he had had a firebreak ploughed around the town as a precaution while Eve cut sandwiches for the firefighters as we sat, watching the bushfire ringing the night sky. 'Will the fires get us?' I asked her. 'No!' Eve said, and I believed her. What Eve said was law.

'Tell us a story, Dad,' we would beg, and Bob would sit us down, wide-eyed, and begin. 'It was a dark and stormy night, and a band of robbers met. The captain said to his mate, "Tell us a bloodthirsty yarn, Dick!" So, Dick sat down and began, "It was a dark and stormy night, and a band of robbers met. The captain said to his mate …' Bob would repeat ad infinitum till we got the joke. He brought a sense to our lives that anything was possible, a sturdy example of someone who found every day interesting, who did not falter in the face of bad luck, bad tidings from the bank, farming disasters, a fire blazing so wildly at the mill that the night sky was racked high and red with smoke for miles around. He got through each day doing his air force exercises, followed by a cold shower and an unshakable sense of right and wrong, no matter who argued differently. Perhaps he grew disappointed, but we did not see it, witnessing firsthand instead his over-whelming ability to make things work and make people work for him. He spoke their language, a working man all his life. When he finally retired, we tried to get him to write the story of his life, but even when we hired a writer to assist him, he could not bring himself to tell any of the secrets he had sworn not to tell. He kept his oath.

The loudest voice in a family of six children born in Broken Hill, Bob was accustomed to the idea of coming first.

'Shut up, you kids!' he would yell at his siblings when his mother had a headache, making it worse with more noise. Determined to make his mark at boarding school in Adelaide, he burnt down the mantlepiece at St Peters College by searing in his initials with a red-hot poker. A champion hurdler and a passionate walker all his life, Bob wrote in notes to himself:

> *I must admit that the moments of perfection seem to me to have been on walking trips and to [have] felt some of the moments I have felt makes it worthwhile to have lived. If there is one way to see the countryside and its people properly it is by walking. To a walker the book of nature is manifest, and all hearts are opened ... he is his own master, he can sing as he likes with no one to castigate him about being out of tune.*

Curious about history and the land, he hiked to Cooper Creek, where Burke and Wills perished:

> *The days spent on this cattle station in the south-western corner of Queensland remain with me because of the men I met there. Truly great men without pretence or pose. Struggling against dust, drought, and death. Able to smile at Nature as*

she bludgeoned them time and again. Wrestling a
living from this bleak inhospitable land. Removed
from all those amenities that seem to make life
worth living and not moaning about it. Truly
great men but unfortunately so few.

In 1943, with twelve months to build the timber industry in Oberon from local hardwoods, Bob had it up and
running in eleven, and when the war ended would take
this up as his business, leaving Broken Hill behind. As a
small child, I would sometimes be allowed to go with him
into the deep virgin forests of the bush where the loggers
were felling timber. The shadows of the Aboriginal ancestors must have haunted those fragrant and secret places,
but the trucks and men stomped around regardless with
huge whining saws. Watching the fall of these giants, I did
not reckon the cost, hypnotised by their majesty and the
beauty all around me flowering in strangely perfumed
shrubs I had never seen before, listening to the whispering wildlife as habitats were destroyed. We did not know
is not enough, but we did not know.

Australia to us was a kind of paradise then, where we were
free to run in the bush, exploring wilderness and farm-
land, running everywhere with Tony, picking mushrooms
and blackberries, shooting snakes, living recklessly till

forced back to boarding school and properly held knives and forks, to silence bells, uniforms, rules and regulations. When we first went to our second boarding school, Marsden, Eve laid our starched blue summer linen tunics flat in the car to keep them uncreased. I was ten and my sister twelve. At the last moment, we donned the tunics and, nervously straightening the seams of our lisle stockings, walked in our black-laced shoes to the majestic front door of the school to meet the formidable headmistress, Miss Appel. Eve held my sister's rubber pillow. 'Mrs Cotton,' Miss Appel remarked coldly, 'your daughter cannot go through life carrying a rubber pillow.' It was the only time I saw Eve visibly wilt. She took the pillow home with her.

*   *   *   *

At sixteen, freed from school, but too young for university, I argued incessantly with Bob and Eve. One day when helping dust, I accidentally dropped and broke the leg off the little glass horse figurine that Eve had watched being blown in Venice, on their trip around the world. When she raged at me, I decided I had had enough and determined to run away from home. Taking my dog, Lisa, and my favourite red parka, I began walking to Sydney, 120 miles away. After I had walked several miles, I saw my father's dark blue Daimler climbing the road towards me and turned around as if headed back home. 'Good idea!' he said, opening the door for me.

*   *   *   *

Bob was handsome and charismatic, a difficult combination, one side of his persona appearing easily accessible, the other surprisingly shy. The more powerful he became, the more he hid that sensitive self behind an easy charisma that seemed to rise from his bones. He climbed through the ranks of the Liberal Party after failing to wrest Macquarie from Chifley in 1949, earning the respect not only of Chifley but also of Robert Menzies for his ability to talk straight in a twisted profession. 'When I come home, I won't be in politics anymore,' he told us. 'I have to tell the prime minister he is wrong.' But Menzies was impressed, and Bob became state president of the NSW Liberal Party from 1957 to 1960, working with John Carrick out of Ash Street. We thought it was a marvellously secretive place, tucked away in the warren of back streets of inner Sydney, a city previously forbidden to us in the grip of the ferocious polio pandemic of the 1940s and early 1950s. Years later, I heard that Bob was nicknamed 'the Kingmaker', carefully placing candidates like chess pieces on the board game of Australia's government.

I watched people fall under his spell. His undertow was magnetic and I started to resist its tidal pull, witnessing the masterclass in charm that was my father making his way in the world. I saw girls and mistresses at boarding school go down in droves when faced with this handsome man in a beret, smoking a pipe with appealing confidence. When I was ten, he came to the school where we were incarcerated and gave me a Bible in front of the fierce headmistress, Miss Appel. He had inscribed the Bible in green ink; *This ink is made from beetles squashed in a teapot*, a very endearing inscription, and I loved him but would not give in, and neither would he. And so began our disagreements that would continue until his years as ambassador for Australia in Washington D.C.

With Australia's involvement in the Vietnam War, and especially when conscription by lottery was introduced in 1964, I had started shouting at my father, 'I would be burning my draft card right now!' And our clashing continued through my disapproval of the Reagan administration with which he was in the United States to negotiate. 'Did you see Caspar?' Eve would ask, after receptions at the Residence, referring to Caspar Weinberger, Reagan's defence secretary. No! I had been avoiding him like the plague, until suddenly face to face one night in front of a Titian painting at the Phillips

Collection, I muttered something in an embarrassed attempt at escape, and he gave me a learned disquisition on the painting and Titian's work in general, forcing me to entertain the notion that he might be human.

Bob left politics in 1978, declaring, 'This game is getting dirty and I'm getting out!' All his life some of his best friends were on the opposite side of the floor. 'I am an Australian, not a Liberal or Labor person,' he remarked. He served as consul general in New York from 1978 to 1981, a year at the Reserve Bank in Australia in 1981 and was then appointed to the ambassadorship from 1982 to 1985. These posts gave him the space to cover the vast territory of Australia's future in the way he felt he could best serve, and he found America energising, loving its sense of reach always impossibly striving to exceed its grasp.

In those last years in America, we made friends again over food fights. Teased relentlessly at lunch one day over hamburgers in a deli, I squirted tomato sauce down his ambassadorial chest. There was a moment of tense silence until he squirted me back. The next day he tipped a plate of pancakes and maple syrup over my head as he passed the breakfast table. We chased each other, squirting mustard, throwing whatever food was at hand until we fell about laughing, the strain of so many years broken at last.

He was born in Broken Hill in 1915 and remembered as a child the sound of rocks being tossed onto the tin roof of his family house on Zebina Street when the miners were on strike. He was a runner and a hurdler and left school at seventeen to help pay for his five siblings' education during the Depression. Robert Carrington Cotton was his name.

When he was two, coming out of church with his mother, Bob saw a rainbow and yelled out, 'Look! There's Gob sliding down the rainbow!' It was his own word for God. The rainbow became his familiar, though I didn't know that till the day he died. What easy joy for Gob to slide down the great arc of colour and light, Joseph's coat of many colours in the sky, just as my father slid down the powerful arc of his life. 'You are so lucky, Bob,' people said to him, which he found insulting: 'I'm not lucky. I work very hard.' And he did too, but he was also lucky, knowing how to walk through an open door when he saw one. In the last months and weeks of his life, losing strength daily, he slid quietly down his rainbow and went to sleep. On the day he died, an otherworldly hand drew great arcs of coloured light wherever I went, a fugitive phenomenon, the de-fraction of sunlight into its component wavelengths, minute droplets of water that hold and transmit light, and I understood that, 'Yes, Gob was sliding down the rainbow.'

VI

1999

It was New Year's Eve, and my sister and I were with our parents in their apartment in Neutral Bay, near where Eve had stayed while she studied at the conservatorium. We were waiting for the century to roll over to 2000. While our husbands drank beer with our father, Eve made tiny finger sandwiches in the kitchen, salmon, and egg with chives. She cut off the crusts. 'Always butter to the edges. Always cut off the crusts!' My sister and I stole and ate the sandwiches as soon as she put them on the plate, and she giggled with delight. She could always summon, but especially at the end, a childlike joy. It was New Year's Eve; therefore, it was wonderful. She could see the fireworks from her window and all the lights reflected in the water of the harbour. Not the best view to be had, but quite good. She stayed up until she had seen the very last of the lights fizz in the air and fall to earth. Eve, the original woman, her night after all. She had lived to see it despite very long odds, lived to see *ETERNITY!* spelt out in lights on the arch of the Sydney Harbour Bridge. Was she waiting for that?

I remembered the explosions of fireworks I had seen as a five-year-old while sitting on a rug on the ground of a park in Sydney under the arch of the bridge. As palm trees swayed overhead, we watched huge bombs of colour burst in the night sky, 26 January 1946, brief imploding stars that fell in long plumes into the salty harbour. I thought it magic. The war was over, Japan having surrendered in September 1945. In my years at Sydney University and later working in the city, I would come across the word *Eternity* written in chalk on footpaths, streets, buildings, the arch of bridges. Going nowhere special, one's feet would suddenly touch *Eternity* on the pavement. At the turn of the century, we felt as if we had touched it again. The story told then was that the word had been written by a woman maddened by the desertion of her husband. But it was written by Arthur Stace, an illiterate former soldier, petty criminal and alcoholic, who became a devout Christian in the late 1940s and turned his attention to writing *Eternity* for thirty-five years all over Sydney.

1996

Morning light in Sydney has a quality of powdered gold, spilt celestial talcum. It gets up the nose. The streets seem to have nothing to think about other than parking and shopping, violence a concept from another hemisphere. The calm seems deliberate, as if events had been smoothed over by a warm knife on pink frosting. Fragrance sheets the air. Walking through it is like wading through a tidal river in bursts of warm and cold.

I was sitting at my father's desk in his study, waiting to call intensive care. Once again, we would drive up the crowded, noisy highway, jostle for parking, walk past the gift-shop baskets of African violets, balloons and stuffed toys. We would sit in the cafeteria, drinking coffee made from wheat instead of coffee beans, eating triangular vegetarian sandwiches – egg and chive, tomato and pickle – the same way we sat for so many days the previous year, waiting for my mother to rouse from a six-week coma after her second heart bypass. It was September, the wattle was flowering, and it smelt like napalm.

The previous night, a baby boy had been born to my niece, and in that one day in September we negotiated the parameters of fear and joy, the anguish of seeing my father lying white and still on a bloodied pillow, as if carved from a huge block of soap, thick plastic tubes snaking away from him, filled with blood. He woke about the same time the baby was born, and our spirits soared. We now saw them both – baby and great-grandfather – as if fleetingly able to grasp both ends of the century at once. That night, jet-lagged and with my head aching, I tiptoed to the kitchen, careful not to wake my mother, and stood looking out at the lights of the city, the bridge, the small toss of dark water where boats rocked in the bay, and thought, they do this, this is how they are here. For a brief period, I was able to see what they saw when they stood there making toast for breakfast. Not without qualms, I slept in my father's bed and used his bathroom. Soon he would return, wobbling in long white surgical stockings, would stand under the shower and feel the soft hot needles of water beat down on his skull. By then I would be gone. I would be standing under my own shower a hemisphere away, with New York's water system raining down on my aching head. My nightmares had come true. The world had split, and my family again gone from sight.

When you return home, you become nameless. You still have the name given to you at birth, but it no longer signifies the person you know. Occasionally you glimpse that self, recognise it slipping around a corner at the mere sight of you. Other people name you as they walk towards you in recognition, but your Self is cancelled; you do not exist in your own form here.

*   *   *   *

At Neutral Bay the ferry rushed in gullying water around shuddering pilings. The harbour smelt of brine and oil. 'I used to take the ferry from here to the conservatorium,' Eve said. 'I used to take my grandmother to town and lead her round. "Step up here. Step down there." She was blind.' I never knew my mother's grandmother was blind. How did that happen? She must have been the one to pay for the conservatorium, as Ollie had no money and Archie drank away any money given him. The story told in the family of my mother's father's mother's mother was that she was 'the first white woman over the Darling River', a pioneer so tough she ruled her station with a stockwhip – husband, sons and Aboriginal people all the same to her. It was also said that when the Aboriginal women were giving birth, Jemima Lydia Hockridge was in their humpies, midwifing the babies. Maybe that's where Eve got her focus on 'the miracle of life', from Jemima Lydia Hockridge, of whom it was claimed that when her husband lay dying, she rode a hundred miles on horseback, without stopping, to reach him. Or that's the story. Which husband? Did she reach him? Surely, she had to change horses. Where did she find a place to do that? I could never hear this story without picturing a stocky woman in late middle age wearing a black buckram dress, her high collar fastened with a large cameo – unyielding, stumpy in the saddle, riding through the cold nights and hot days, accumulating dust and mud on her black dress while regret accumulated along her rigid spine. I would imagine her riding the horse grim-faced till it dropped, muzzle covered in foam, her clothing damp with sweat and dirt, steel grey hair faltering in the wind from the pinioning bun. I am glad political correctness never arrived in time to dim her iron core. How many horses did she kill? Did she get there in time?

*   *   *   *

Letter to me from Eve, 25 June 1972:

> *For some weeks now I have been doing some occasional research into my (and your) family history. The great-grandmother I have mentioned to you is Jemima Lydia Hockridge who married Thomas McGeorge in 1849. The catch is her surname in some documents is*

given as Hockridge, then Hockridge Geake and then this morning just Geak. So that's going to be interesting to unravel. I have found some contractors, a domestic, a baker and praise be, this morning – a gentleman named John Campbell Macdougall, occupation 'Gentleman'!! His wife was Marie Butler and their son one of my grandfathers, was Ormond Campbell Macdougall and one of his sons Ormond Butler Macdougall. So, you can see I have many leads on that line.

Jemima Lydia Hockridge (Geake) was born in 1831, in Exeter, Devonshire. Married (as Hockridge) in 1849 to Thomas McGeorge. Married (again) in 1869 (as J.L. Hockridge Geake McGeorge) to William Kenavan, the mayor of Wilcannia. Died in Bourke – her father's name is given as Geake. She was seventy-three.

1982

Eve's disaffection for Jean somehow extended to the Harradines, their mother's side of the family, so that Eve only cared about her father's Scottish ancestry. 'I am a *Macdougall*,' she explained proudly, 'from the Campbell line.' She began to research the family. 'You are not Scottish, your blood is polluted by your father's English blood,' she explained to my sister and me. It was all about bloodlines, the stud breeder always at work, even after my father sold the farm on the way to Washington in 1982. It made Eve very angry. 'I know what your father does,' she said, 'but what do I do?' Her sheep were sold along with the stud books and their musical scores of bloodlines, one crossed with another until the third looked better than the two who had produced it. Eve was breeding for 'better lines', a complicated equation she could do in her head whenever she looked at 'her girls'. But my father had reached such a level that she had no choice but to follow him and be the hostess that diplomacy required. Given the Washington establishment to run and a heavy calendar of entertaining, she nearly died of a heart attack instead. She expected to die at sixty-four, my father told me when she died at eighty-three years and twenty-two days. She had better bloodlines than she knew, but it took two bypass operations to get her there.

*   *   *   *

Births registered in	New South Wales, Australia
Certified copy furnished under	Part V of the *Registration of Births, Deaths and Marriages Act 1973*
Issued at	Sydney, 10 March 1982
Date and place of birth of child	5 July 1917, William Street
Name and whether present or not	Eve Elizabeth (not present)
Gender	female
Father's name, occupation, age and birthplace	Archibald Campbell Macdougall, agent, 34 years, Adelaide, South Australia
Date and place of marriage – previous issue	15 January 1913, Church Hill, Sydney, NSW, Jean M. H. – living. None deceased.
Mother's name and maiden surname, age and birthplace	Olive Harradine, 26 years, West Maitland, NSW
Informant	Olive Macdougall, mother
Witnesses	Dr. Robertson and Nurse Field
Particulars of Registration	O.E.A., 4 September 1917

I, John Brettell Holliday, hereby certify that the above is a true copy of particulars recorded in a register. Signed J.B. Holliday, Principal Registrar

*   *   *   *

Looking through the papers Eve sent, I found a note to me in her careful handwriting: *[the] Crest: lion's paw holding a dagger – Mcdougall or Macdougall – Scotland. A lion's gamb raised and erect, holding a dagger.'* FORTIS IN ARDUIS. Fortis *means 'strongly articulated' and* arduis *means 'steep or difficult' or 'strength in difficulties'. 'Strength in adversity'*, clearly what Eve inherited.

> I remember it so clearly. My father wore a
> three-sided gold fob on his watch chain and
> when he died, it was given to Jean as the elder.
> However, she lost or sold it. She hated her father
> so much she probably sold it. My mother had
> the same feeling and when he died, she burnt
> all the papers and in particular I remember two
> portraits – one of my father the other his mother.
> So, I have nothing to work from other than bits of
> memory and B. D. & M. certificates.

John Macdougall, Eve's favourite ancestor, was a high-spirited ship owner who sank his ship, reputed to be carrying sugar and coffee with no one aboard, for the insurance money. He was convicted and sent to Van Diemen's Land with his wife and five children. He applied for a pardon, somehow got one, and became a publican. It was said he then ran a newspaper with his son John

Campbell Macdougall. They had a place at Pittwater, the calm saltwater side of the peninsula in the Pacific that is Palm Beach. This was where we went every Christmas holiday and rode the ferry it is rumoured he had something to do with starting. Eve had two other convict ancestors sent to Australia for taking part in the Irish Rebellion – Ann Roberts and Lawrence Butler – the unacknowledged Irish in her bloodlines.

*   *   *   *

It turned out that we did have an uncle (Ormond) Butler. He replaced Eve's grandmother's rubies and emeralds with paste, and when Ollie tried to sell them needing money, she discovered they were fake. 'I used to try them on when I was a child,' Eve said, regret sharp in her voice. 'The emerald was to go to Jean when my grandmother died, but the ruby was mine. It was in the shape of a bee, and I used to wear it as a child.' Was Bebe named for it? Did any of the jewellery my father bought her during their long years together make up for that first disappointment? 'I am leaving you my rubies,' she told me, not long before she died. 'Please don't,' I replied. I hated them. 'Just leave me the little star sapphire earrings.' They spoke to me of her. She bought them in Cairo in 1955 when my parents had sailed on the SS *Oronsay* taking a six-month trip to England, Europe and the United States as good colonials did at the time. One of the first stops was Cairo, after the Suez Canal, and when Eve saw the small blue ovals held in a rim of tiny gold leaves, she knew they were hers. 'Eight pounds,' the shopkeeper demanded. 'Too much for fakes,' my father said, not believing they were real. But Eve, Bebe the Wheedler, loved them, so he paid eight pounds, and she wore them with careless pleasure. Assessed twenty years later, they were found to be star sapphires. She wore them in New York as the consul general's wife, living in a fancy duplex apartment that overlooked the East River, with three maids, a cook, a car, and a driver. She considered this the way she deserved to live and enjoyed New York intensely; it was her kind of town. She still had her sheep but ran the farm from afar through managers. While it had been successful enough to break even before they left, it now began to lose money without her careful daily handling.

Bob loved everything about New York: the slow barges wrinkling the East River, the trademark – 'How'm I doin'? – of its brash and tenacious mayor, Ed Koch, the Pepsi-Cola sign that glowed across the river from their apartment, Runyon's pub, the dealmakers and high rollers. His office was on the fourth floor of the Rockefeller Centre, with a view of Fifth Avenue and below the statue

of Atlas holding up the world in bronze just across from
St Patrick's. From there he watched parades, and if he
sometimes felt that he too was holding up the world, it
never showed. Death threats, anonymous and otherwise,
rolled right off him, and he kept walking home every day
for lunch despite them, along the city streets he loved.
Before returning to the United States again in 1982, my
father sold the house, both farms, the Hampshire Down
stud sheep and the Murray Grey cattle. 'It's too cold for
your mother,' he explained guiltily, 'she has arthritis.' Eve
worked up a good set of arterial blockages in preparation
for a massive heart attack. She had talent and she used
it. The heart attack was averted by a surgeon who took
veins from her legs, cracked open her chest and sewed
them in place of her diseased arteries.

*   *   *   *

Bob and Eve were now posted to Washington, and I flew
down to be present for Eve's angiogram, after which the
surgeon told us he planned to keep her in hospital for a
week before the bypass operation. I beckoned him outside the hospital door. 'Yes?' the surgeon said, raising his
eyebrow, a tall medical god in a white coat. 'You will oper-
ate on this patient at seven a.m. tomorrow,' I said, and
after more demanding on my part, he agreed. Walking

towards my father and me in his green scrubs after the operation, he described the five-hour triple bypass he had performed on Eve, then turned to me and asked, 'Are you from New York?' Yes, I was, and no, I wasn't. I had learnt how to be brash; I knew my mother, and he didn't.

*   *   *   *

Slumped in a vinyl chair, her hospital gown wrenched around with half-tied strings, Eve lay suspended between life and death. The machines to which she was hooked beat with a steady umbilical pulse – click, breathe, click, breathe – as oxygen hurried down the clear plastic tube in each nostril, clipped onto the inherited nose she had always so disliked: 'It should have been better!' In the Washington hospital that seemed as exhausted as she did, I watched the furious heartbeats shake her body, heaving her ribs as if to explode the organ from its narrow housing. The little green lights on the heart monitor blipped across the screen, numbers changing continually – 100, 102, 99, 86, 96, 98, 97, 88, 4, 100 – as if unable to make up their mind. Eve was in limbo beyond reach, struggling to recover from the triple bypass. This challenged their long marriage, with Bob managing the nation's embassy in a foreign land and hating having to witness Eve unconscious. When she did not respond to him, he brought balloons and released them to float on the ceiling of her hospital room. 'How could either of them cope without the other? They are together!' said one of her friends. 'What would your father do?'

Where was Eve wandering? Through the corridors of the grand ambassadorial residence, explaining to the maid, Umpey, that the guest room had to be prepared for a visiting prime minister who had requested a hair dryer, or arranging for George, the butler, to assist at a formal dinner in his bee-striped jacket, or ordering Santino, the cook, to prepare for a reception? Maybe she was wondering one more time if I had finally met Caspar Weinberger or was still dodging him. Perhaps she was back in Broken Hill in delirium, her ten-year-old neck encased in plaster, or perhaps cleaning the red powder from the pantry after a dust storm. Maybe she was at the farm in Oberon, wielding command over what lived and died in her pianist's hands. As I watched her tiny figure struggle to return to consciousness, I remembered how she would bring limp lambs, orphaned, or deserted by their mothers, into the kitchen and drag them back to life on the heated floor with bottles of colostrum and regular bottle feedings. She paid passionate attention to their survival, and afterwards they were tame to her touch. I tried to bring that same attention to force her to live.

When the farm was sold, Eve grieved deeply. 'The farm was what I do!' she said, full of hurt, anger and resentment, but my father's career ran now in high octane elsewhere, and the cash continually seeping into the bottomless pit of farming cost her hers. I remembered that when Eve and Bob had returned from their world trip in 1955, she had come down the gangway doing something unusual for her – singing. 'Oh, look at me! Oh, look at me, I'm dancing!' They had just been to the new musical *Salad Days* in London, and this was its theme song. She was so happy. Was she ever that happy again? I tried to sing it to her in hospital. I asked her who she was, who I was, I asked her what was my dog's name? Finally, through the intense fog of pain and anaesthetic, her chest carved open then closed with clips, came the laboured, slowly gasped response: 'Spot.' My dog's name was Spike, but I knew this was her attempt at humour. At last, she was coming back from the brink.

*   *   *   *

Courtesy of the Australian government, Bob and Eve now lived in high style in Washington D.C. in a grand residence on Cleveland Avenue, which was built in 1926 and had a garden so beautiful they gave parties to celebrate its two hundred azaleas blooming in different colours. Eve had gone with Bob to the White House, wearing her white gloves and hat, when he presented his credentials to the inflexibly charming and absent-minded president. I disagreed with everything Reagan did of course. It was now a habit with me. When Bob took me to the White House Rose Garden to celebrate Australia's win in the 1983 America's Cup, I seemed to easily disconcert George H.W. Bush when I was introduced to him, but when Reagan walked into the garden, I found to my horror that the force of his charisma was such that I was drawn towards him. Or was it the aura of power that surged along with him?

*   *   *   *

Eve did not like wet footprints beside the swimming pool at the Cleveland residence if guests were to come. Her sense of impeccable order was offended by them, so she would not have opened the front door when one morning the butler, George, saw through the glass panes a man's naked chest when he heard knocking. He assumed my husband, Yale, or my son had gone swimming and locked themselves out. We were all staying at the Residence for Thanksgiving, including Yale's formidable mother, whose ancestors had come over to America on the *Mayflower*. When George opened the door, a man stood there, holding a fan, his kimono dropped to the ground.

As George rushed inside to phone the police, the naked intruder raced upstairs to the bedrooms. What followed perfectly described the Residence's inhabitants. My father came out, saw that the police had everything under control, and went to work in his home office. Eve came out and followed the police down the long corridor of guest bedrooms, fascinated by the mayhem. My mother-in-law, who believed it bad manners to touch one's feet or hair in public, stayed in her room, not prepared to open the door, and add to the noise and confusion. My son, Tim, rolled over in bed, heard the police, decided all was under control, and went back to sleep. As I groggily struggled to enter our bathroom, my husband held me back. I thought a blaring television had been left on. But no, the intruder had made it to the bathroom, where he was drawing on the mirror with soap bubbles as the police tried to handcuff him and take him back to the facility from which he had escaped. It was Thanksgiving, so that night Eve and Bob had Thanksgiving dinner sent to him at the asylum.

*　　　　*　　　　*　　　　*

As the new Australian ambassador, Bob was required to pay a visit to the dean of the diplomatic corps in Washington, who was then the Russian ambassador, Anatoly

Fyodorovich Dobrynin. 'How much do they pay you?' Dobrynin asked Bob. 'Enough,' he answered. 'Do you know how much they pay me?' Dobrynin asked him. 'I am paid twelve hundred dollars.' And Bob replied, 'That's not bad.' Dobrynin responded, 'Twelve hundred dollars a year! But I can spend all I want on food and entertaining.' He proceeded to stuff himself with vast quantities of the expensive food laid out as required by his senior diplomatic status.

1999

I have returned yet again to the land of parrots and powdery gold skies. I wander through local shops, looking at cold meat pies and sausage rolls with thick lard crusts, at mangoes, mushrooms, pumpkins, lettuce, spinach, oranges – everything in the familiar shops feels and smells so different from my life in the northern hemisphere. The fragrance of tuberose, freesia, jasmine and lilies court my memory, and I become eighteen again in a white dress with stripes of red cherries around the full skirt and a wide red belt, in love with the world, considering an engagement to a handsome man my mother has deemed a dilettante. Despite her we will marry in 1961. He is six years older than me and will become a diplomat and the father of my only child, a son born in New Zealand in 1963. The marriage lasted seven years, the divorce took longer.

I stop in Hyde Park to watch the familiar fountain and the entitled ibises stalking about on long-legged black feet. I remember eating thin chicken sandwiches, with their crusts cut off, nearby in David Jones with Ollie: 'Always butter to the edges. Always cut off the crusts.' It was here I last saw Tony, leaning against the wall, just after he had volunteered for Vietnam and was training to be a pilot.

The park uncoils with memories of him, young and handsome in his uniform, expecting the world.

When I go to see my mother later in Neutral Bay, I pass along an avenue of jacarandas on McDougall Street, flowering with a violet jolt against the ultramarine harbour. Lilac spills onto the ground underfoot and arches overhead, turning the light from flat blue to luminous purple. Nearby, my mother lies in bed. When Eve complains to me about pain, about her rapid heartbeat, about tiredness that makes her life a struggle, it makes me feel ill. I squirm as if long, thin, hot needles were stuck into me in a thousand places at once and am unable to turn away, breathe or escape. I feel her complaints in my bones, flesh of her flesh. When she cannot sleep, she takes a pill. 'How did you sleep?' I ask. 'I died,' Eve responds, with pleasant malice.

2000

It is 23 May 2000, and I have been called to my mother's bedside again. On the last day of this trip home, I hurry down the long sweep of Awaba Street in Mosman, which empties precipitously into the blue Pacific. I watch the glittery swash of small waves on the north half of white sand curved to meet its double in the middle, Balmoral Beach, where I escape whenever I can to swim and stare out to sea. Last night a three-quarter moon cut a coppery path between the middle and south heads that slid to the door of my room, beckoning to where my husband and small old white-faced dog, Spike, wait on the other side of the world. In a different hemisphere, I will watch the same moon and wonder how many more days my mother might live, her tiny bones under my hand, her neck frail from the weight of her head that wobbles like a newborn, hair lovingly dried and curled by her hairdresser, Mitch, who works in his off hours as a drag queen, Ms Patsy de Kline. Often when I enter my mother's room in the hospital, she is sleeping, her face holding some secret, tightly enclosed place I cannot go. I long to be in the air and away from feeling.

I leave again. 'No worries,' says the hostess, handing me a drink. The sun is setting, low and hazy, a pink-gold cut off abruptly at dusk. At my sister's house, birds would be gathering in a twittering chatter, swooping, and streaking past to focus, like grains of metal to a magnet, in the old Moreton Bay figs on the Esplanade. My life has no resonance here now, rendered invisible by distance. 'There is a row of lights on the floor to guide you in the event of darkness or smoke,' the hostess tells the cabin. 'You can make the oxygen flow simply by pulling the tab marked *Pull*. Extra air can be added by this mouthpiece and the jacket has a light and a whistle for attracting attention. Thank you for watching. Your safety is our priority.' My hands are hot and my back hurts. There are twelve directional lights on my seat: up, down, footrest, back cushion, music, movie, call hostess.

Will she be alive when I return in two months? I have cleaned out her closet as she wished, bringing an item of clothing each day for her inspection, and saw clearly on her face, despite our laughter, the understanding that we are readying her to die. 'Don't hurry me,' she says to me, two days before her actual death. But this time, the second-to-last time, she gives me a pair of her shoes, bright-red suede Valentino flats with big bows. Maybe she thinks I will wear them; we have the same size feet. But I think she has given me Dorothy's ruby slippers, and when I am far away, living in the other half of the world – days, nights, seasons reversed – I will look at them, click the heels together and say, 'There's no place like home.'

How will I live without her frail, ironclad spirit determining that I wear this not that, should or shouldn't say this, should eat this: 'a little sugar is good for you'. Sitting in the sunshine in a wheelchair, Eve's face changes, her eyes blazing with sudden brightness as she talks about her beloved crosswords. 'Lateral thinking,' she says to me of them, wearing the lavender dressing-gown I had given her, which she loves so much she wears it in bed while unravelling puzzle clues. My sister and I wheel her around the circle of the hospital drive to see her favourite brilliant yellow Macaulay rose, then back to her room, where I massage her feet. 'Give me a hug,' she says, and I wrap my arms around the tiny, complete structure of 83-year-old bones barely hinged together that is still my mother and know that later I will feel real pain.

The engines are revving, and the plane slowly backs out. When I rang my father from the airport, he said that he was going to rest and then go for a walk. 'Don't go out too late,' I say. 'It's getting dark early.' Into that gathering dark, the plane pulls out. It lifts into a parrot sky, a scream of crimson slashing grey clouds, a trace of orange stripe on the horizon. Below there is harbour water, a sprinkle of yellow headlights, traffic going home. We turn out to sea. The lights fade from sight. I leave again. As the plane levels out over the Pacific, I slump in my seat and feel as if the marrow has been sucked from my bones by the glittering island I have left behind, its hungry people reciting a rosary of their existence, as if leaving something unsaid, they might disintegrate and fall off the edge of this continent constantly eroded by waves. No matter how far I go, it holds me convict and prisoner.

*   *   *   *

It is July 2000, and Eve's illness has turned inexorably to its final stage. I have returned to Sydney's seaside suburbs, grown rich and buttery with Mercedes and BMWs. The morning opens to a guttural whine of leaf-blowers, scolding foliage and flowers dropped carelessly overnight onto springy lawns. Later, there is an oppressive quiet, the stubborn calm broken occasionally by the harsh squeak of a parrot or children playing. It is difficult to believe that anything happens here. People marry, give birth and die, but it seems impossible; the country too tidily restrained by its perimeter of long, flat-topped sandstone cliffs patrolled by the blue Pacific, making escape so impossible and an ideal penal colony nearly three hundred years ago.

At dawn the sun bursts from the clouds with a shout of apricot, gilding the house and rinsing the gunmetal sea. The air is quiet as honey. The ocean has goosebumps, the edge of the land is a pale whitish gold, the rim of the continent slowly eroding, and always the tireless sound of the sea, an ancient island's rasping breath.

Four cockatoos sit on the railing of my sister's house, stretching their lemony wings. The coal cuckoo strikes a single note like a clock. A pair of butcherbirds come to the verandah that overlooks Balmoral, flying so fast they catch meat thrown in mid-air. Below, a rock is struggling with the tide like a swimmer, the sea shivering in filmy layers as if it were sheer fabric pulled diagonally in ruched pleats, one across the other, sewing a gown by Fortuny even more beautiful than the one Eve had made in Colombo.

Briefly the sky grows dark, cracked with pale orange and heavy as a lid. A coppery brightness hangs over tiled rooftops. Light skids off the beaten pewter ocean furrowed with the silver scars of boat wakes, like fish skeletons etched on mother-of-pearl. At the edge of the horizon, a huge tanker looms and black water rinses the headlands. Rocks that mark the edge of the land rise in and out of the swells. The silent house ticks.

Before I arrived, my sister wrapped our mother in a rug, drove her to North Head and pushed her wheelchair to the edge of the cliff, so that Eve could take her last deep breaths of the Pacific. The waves poured out the rhythm of her requiem, rolling one over the other to crash on rocks below. She watched a small brown-gold hawk dodge and wheel around the cliff face, saw swallows and wrens, smelt native flowering shrubs, felt the sunlight on her face, sat and observed her life distil into these perfect final chords. When I arrived two days later, Eve was in a hospital bed. 'I thought you'd come sooner,' she said, having sternly forbidden me to come. 'Rub my feet, please.'

*   *   *   *

Nightfall here is freighted with noise, a crescendo of birdcall that squeaks and grates. Lorikeets flash past in a screech of rainbow feathers. The air is tropical, flowers and fruit phantoms from the past, aroma indelible. Fruit bats creak busily in the huge Moreton Bay fig trees. The roots drop from their branches like mangroves searching for water. Standing on the small upstairs balcony, I look out at the broken path of the moon, where a wide boat wake curves to veer out of the Heads and melt into the Pacific. The water under the dark jetty at Balmoral quavers with striped light. A little ripple of sea folds its edge neatly over on the curve of sand. The strand of net lacing the north half of the beach to the island in the middle is studded with birds: black-and-white pelicans, cormorants with wings spread to dry. When I return in later years, the net will be gone. The house lights glow like luminous wild blooms, and an owl hoots unexpectedly. I've never heard one before. My mother is dying, maybe tonight, maybe tomorrow, and I want to follow the path of the moon and escape.

*   *   *   *

She died on Thursday, 27 July 2000, at noon exactly, as my niece Amanda sang Giordani's arietta 'Thou, All My Bliss' ('*Caro Mio Ben*') in a clear voice: 'Thou, all my bliss, believe but this: when thou art far, my heart is lorn. Believe but this: when thou art far, my heart is lorn.'

As her coffin was carried from the church, the organ played Bach's 'Sheep May Safely Graze'. I choked up when I heard it. 'I carried Mere,' my young grandnephew

Tim said proudly, having held onto the handles of her coffin as it made its way down the aisle to the hearse. 'Yes, you did,' I replied. 'Yes, you did.' At the crematorium, his mother, Jo, suddenly stepped up and, taking a handle of the coffin from one of the men, carried Eve's body to the flames. Her fierce courage brought tears to my eyes.

*   *   *   *

Storing food in clear plastic containers does not save your life. My mother organised all her food in them: cereal, beans, apricots, oatmeal, pasta, dried tomatoes, porcini, split peas, tea bags, raisins, crackers, nuts. The potato chips she had each night with a brandy while watching the news – 'The doctor says I can!' – were kept in a clear plastic jar stored in the cabinet by her hospital bed. Eve organised dying like a fine piano concerto. 'The bed jacket must go on the right-hand side with the clean nightgowns, the dirty ones on the left. I like the green one best. Please wash it now and make sure you hang it to drip-dry, otherwise it will crease. Don't put it in the dryer.' She died anyway.

Eve told the truth. How she did this is beyond me. When most women tell the truth, they do so with a certain defiance, expecting to be set alight at the stake. Eve did it with a pertinent charm that was devastating: 'Your skin is too sallow for orange.' 'Horizontal stripes are unkind to your hips.' 'Oh dear, not grey again.' She commented on inappropriate clothing, husbands and haircuts, on roots showing, a vase of flowers or world news not arranged to her liking. She pecked at tiny flaws and big ones, a hen in the yard after grain, a pianist aiming for precisely the right note.

*   *   *   *

The Sydney Morning Herald

EVE COTTON

Australian heroine 1917–2000

Australia has a tradition, at once grand and humble, of remarkable women who never sought the limelight for themselves but provided the foundations upon which were built brilliant careers and illustrious families. Lady (Eve) Cotton, who has died in Sydney aged 83, was one of those women.

Born in Broken Hill in 1917, Eve Elizabeth Macdougall (she would become known as Mere to her family and Eve to her friends) was a pianist of sufficient talent to take a place at the Sydney Conservatorium. She also became known as Cousin Eve on 2BH radio's 'Children's Hour'.

At the age of 20 she married Robert Carrington Cotton in Broken Hill and they honeymooned in Ceylon, now Sri Lanka. In retrospect, this dynamic contrast set a pattern for their 63 years of marriage. It took them from comfortable anonymity in rural NSW to the inner political circles of Canberra and on to distinguished diplomacy for Australia in Washington and New York. This partnership ended last week when Lady Cotton died peacefully in the care of her family after a final long illness.

In many respects, her life reflected the 20th century, encompassing its changes and upheavals – from her own birth in the climatic year of World War I, and then as a young wife and mother, she volunteered to serve as a truck driver in the World War II.

When, in the postwar boom years, her husband's business and the federal political career gathered pace, it was her successful negotiation of that difficult terrain of mother of three and rurally based wife of an often-absent partner that was the unseen cornerstone of Bob Cotton's achievement.

It was not a one-career family, however. Eve became one of the most successful sheep breeders in the Southern Hemisphere. Her Oberon stud farm produced some of the finest Hampshire Downs stock ever to win blue ribbons at Sydney's Royal Easter Show. In her personal life, her sense of perfection, and attention to detail were legendary, as was her wit.

She also maintained a lifelong passion for music, science, world events, tumultuous weather, crosswords, politics, people and – above all – her family.

Her three children were encouraged from the earliest age to do what they felt they must. For her artist daughters, Anne Ferguson and Judy Cotton, this meant early creative practice on the walls and furniture of their bedrooms. As a small boy, her son, Robert, showed precocious diplomatic skills in dealing with his elder sisters and has followed his parents into distinguished service for Australia overseas. Cotton's seven grandchildren and three great-grandchildren also experienced the steadfast love of this remarkable woman.

The Cotton's more than six decades of marriage encompassed early struggles, parenthood, the timber industry, politics, farming, sandstorms, bushfires, drought, booms and slumps – and a knighthood conferred at Buckingham Palace.

Respected on both sides of politics, they enhanced Australia's standing when Bob was appointed consul general in New York and then ambassador in Washington. Nevertheless, Eve was always a modest and private person, and was overjoyed to return to her beloved Sydney.

In later years, as her health began to fail, her spirit, grace and courage did not. Her mind was the most pertinent and particular of features. She informed herself and informed those around her. She had a wonderful sense of fun and she had great style.

She loved and gave unstintingly, and her lasting legacy is the loving and distinguished family she built and now leaves behind to celebrate and mourn her.

Diana Simmonds
5 August 2000

*   *   *   *

We found this in a book of Eve's after she died:

EULOGY

Do not stand by my grave and weep

I am not there. I do not sleep.

I am a thousand winds that blow,

I am a diamond glint on snow,

I am the sunlight on ripened grain,

I am the gentle autumn rain.

When you awaken in the morning hush

I am the swift uplifting rush

Of quiet birds in circling flight.

I am the soft starshine at night.

Do not stand by my grave and cry

I am not there

I did not die.

*   *   *   *

A letter from Shirley Hazzard, who knew Bob and Eve in
New York, 10 August 2000:

Dear Judy

*I just received your letter. I think of all the letters
you must be answering about this beloved and
delightful woman. The obituary is beautiful, if
I may say so, and give us her radiance. Your
parents, who shared so much with each other,
shared with their friends, and with the world,
the precious quality of generosity: generosity of
heart and spirit, a generous intelligence. Your
mother was intuitive, fastidious, thoughtful, and
tactful, as well as immeasurably kind. How much
laughter, too, they brought to life, those dear
people. How grateful I am to have them in my
consciousness forever.*

*Grateful, too, for the last time I saw them. When
I was in Sydney three years ago, they asked
me to lunch at the restaurant in Balmoral Cove,
near the old Baths. They'd chosen the place
knowing that I grew up at Balmoral and went to
Queenwood School. What an experience it was,
to sit there with Eve and Bob, looking out at
the Heads with double vision – because every*

*rock was familiar, the light was itself childhood
revisited: yet I saw it all with a fresh eye, a visitor
discovering beauty.*

*I feel very deeply for your father. No one knows,
without encountering it, the loss of the beloved
companion: terrible, incomparable, yet infinitely
precious. One would not forgo, even if one could,
the pain, because in that one remains close.*

*The loss of Eve comes – as these losses tend
to do – in a series of extraordinary departures
of recent weeks: our long and dear friend the
writer William Maxwell died three weeks ago,
one week after his beautiful wife Emily. All these
irreplaceable people – one has been immensely
fortunate in knowing them.*

*Dear Judith, I think of your loving presence in
your parent's life – your devotion to your mother
in her illnesses, and your vital companionship in
her existence. The SMH article speaks of her joy
in her daughter's creativity – and how proud she
was of your gift, your work. How much happiness
there is in all this.*

*With love to you both,
Shirley*

P.S. I smiled at the SMH mention of sheep, and I remember her 'collection' …

Shirley saw the public Eve, who had worked 'at making things go well'. She did not see the other Eve, who thought 'things should have been better', the Eve who would turn her face away or cut it from photographs and close the piano to encompass silence.

*   *   *   *

'Jean was the beautiful one,' Eve said. 'It was Jean everyone looked at.' Jean was the sister whose effortless charm was so practised she grew cavalier about using it to get whatever and wherever she wanted. Jean was the one who had held a living bird of paradise in her hands and stroked its brilliant plumage. It was Jean who smoked and drank, and adventured into the tropical world of New Guinea, with a hibiscus behind her ear, far beyond anyone's reach. But if Eve had read her own obituary, would she feel that she, Bebe, the younger sister, had won? Or would she still be the thwarted married pianist who felt that she would never have been as good as she should have been. Jean and Eve each had remarkable abilities, but Eve mastered hers with careful precision, and was celebrated at the end for a life of achievement. Jean threw her talent to the winds of chance, expecting her gifts to go on forever. 'She had so much talent and she wasted it,' said Eve, who played out her own life with the restrained passion of a piano prodigy, producing a full concerto, not a note wasted. Was she content with this, with the passages and cadenzas that would mark her days? What would scarlet Jean have thought of her younger sister's remarkable obituary; Jean, the aunt I barely knew, but whose wildness I secretly found inspiring? Jean would have lit another cigarette and tossed her red hair in the direction of a likely man at the bar. She did not have to acknowledge her younger sister's triumph, for Jean was already dead.

I have a photograph of Eve and Jean on a beach as young women. Eve's body looks full and vulnerable. She turns from the camera, shy and mistrustful, while Jean, holding a big straw hat, laughs at the camera with her big white teeth. She laughs at the sky, at the whole earth making room for her. It was a lie. There was no room.

*   *   *   *

As I waited for my divorce to come to trial in 1970, my father, with whom I now disagreed on every issue, took me to see Jean and her latest young lover. I knew this was an object lesson aimed at me – I was supposed to take a good look at Jean, the only person in the family to be divorced, and realise who I might become. At the last moment, Eve had a headache and could not come with us. She always had a headache at the last moment. Jean lived in a cheap little house in Botany Bay under the flight path of the Kingsford Smith airport, and it smelt of jet fuel, not the sea. After so many years in the sun in New Guinea and Queensland, Jean was deeply tanned. She had thatched the roof of the tiny back verandah with dried palm fronds. It looked like a seedy tropical bar, and as we sat on it, sipping drinks with her latest young man, Jean seemed deeply nervous. She asked my father for a favour: a job for the young man, an introduction, money. We were all embarrassed. My father gave it, of course. He always did, just as he made clear without words, as if using a pointer on a map, that this was the way female flesh fell to rock bottom, and if I were not careful, I would find myself under a thatched roof in a cheap suburb, begging for help. Jean's big white teeth were stained yellow from years of cigarettes. Her hair was dyed as red as her nails. She looked brave and awful under the whistling palm thatch. Later, I realised her big smile held more than a hint of panic, but by then I too was divorced.

I hope Jean got good and stinking after that meeting. We had spelt out, in the way we parsimoniously sipped at our unwanted drinks, that we trod the road of the righteous, that her failure could be contagious, and that we would wash carefully afterwards.

Years later, I heard Jean had moved back to Queensland, to Gympie, where she had been found comatose in a bathtub in 1947, scalding water dripping onto her left foot. The third-degree burn had left a coffee-coloured pucker on her ankle. She had not been comatose but dead drunk, and Eve had hurriedly flown north to 'tidy her up'. Later, Bob and Eve built a house for Jean in Gympie that she so loved. Whenever she needed money, my father paid. I used to wonder why he did this when Eve had so little time for her. Now I know he paid because it's what family does.

For a while Jean was quiet with her mangoes and passionfruit vines, the little sandy garden of flowers outlined in seashells. Then her neighbours started calling Bob and Eve. 'Jean is using the garden as a bathroom!' they said, through pursed lips that echoed down the long-distance phone line. Again, my mother flew north. Jean was hospitalised with throat cancer and other problems, not the least of which was the joy she took pooping in her garden, scratching dirt with dusty, cracked feet over the long, stinky coils. When Jean died, they called it 'a hardening of the arteries' along with throat cancer. I imagined a wilting red hibiscus in a glass of water by Jean's hospital bed. No red lipstick, no scarlet fingernails holding a cigarette, just red dye retreating from the roots of her hair until a frosty halo rimmed her skull.

Jean's funeral was one more thing I wasn't there for. I did not see the wooden coffin slide into the flames, or her ashes being placed in a metal box in a blank concrete wall. What is the name on the metal plate? Mrs Jean Wilson, the married woman she had long ago ceased to be, or Jean Mina Macdougall, Ollie and Archie's girl? *She has a nice view now*, my father wrote. What did he mean? Do ashes watch the sea? Eve was sick and could not attend the funeral. She had a headache. She had pneumonia. She had hurt her knee. Her foot was poisoned. Her pulse was too rapid; one of those things. She did not see her sister turned into ash and locked into a small metal box with a view of the sea.

VII

It is 5 April 2001, and I am here, one day past my birthday, one year after Eve's death. The air is soft and full of eucalypt. Now there is no one to tell me how long I took to be born, how much I had resisted. 'Two days and you wouldn't get started. They had to pack me with towels. Then you were born blue, choked by the cord around your neck. The doctor had lost his son the same way the week before, so he snatched the cord away and you lived.' It seemed she never forgave me for that excruciating childbirth, holding a grudge her entire life.

I go to the apartment to see my father, who has just had a pacemaker put in. He seems frail, but pinker and less forgetful. He unlocks the safe and gives me Eve's watch, and I am struck by the vividness of this life lived, now gone. It seems I barely knew her yet know her with each breath. I turn my wrist to show my father the watch, and it looks like my mother's wrist turning. They bought the Piaget watch together in 1969 in Switzerland. They had just come from the Soviet Union, then under Brezhnev's grip, where the Politburo had tried to bully my father, now Minister for Civil Aviation. But he had returned the attack with such animated vigour that he impressed them. 'You were very good, Bob,' Eve told him, enjoying the champagne and caviar, ballet tickets, private tours, and fresh orange juice the Kremlin kept sending them. Now, Eve wanted a watch – a good one. In Switzerland, she looked at the tray of expensive watches and explained to the salesman the very different roles she was expected to manage, politician's wife, stud-breeding farmer, mother, grandmother. 'Then this is the watch for you, madam,' he said, holding up a blue-faced platinum one with small diamonds around the rim. 'Yes, this is the watch,' Eve replied, content. The watch's face has turned black and makes me sad, as does the sight of her shower cap still hanging beside her shower, as if it had just shed water from its lace edging. Her breath still seems to rise and fall in these rooms, and I expect to find an unfinished crossword by her side of the bed, where a rose sits in a little crystal vase, just as it did every day of her final years, a tribute from my father. Everything is redolent of her determination. 'The fruit must go in this bowl here, on this counter. The tea must be in the blue-and-white cups. We must eat on the terrace with these placemats, and the salt and pepper go here.' Her orchids are beginning to flower. My father treats them as carefully as if she could see them. A year later, he married again.

I wash my hands in her bathroom, stung by the smell of her soap, drying my hands on the towels she found to be not exactly the right colour, not a good enough match with the bathmat. It is easy to say that it breaks my heart, but it does. I walk by her garden, which has the big stone pots holding her favourite camellias. Eve's determination seems lodged in these creviced pots, which she insisted be carried from the enclosed garden at the farm to the first house at the beach, then the second house at the beach, and finally this last place, an apartment that overlooks the harbour, which she felt was never exactly right. The view could have been better. 'It would be better if there were sun. It would be better if the gardener would prune the trees harder and open the view. It would be better if the apartment block to one side were not there. It would be better if one did not see that long thin metal exhaust chimney. It would be better if.'

I go to the bank, to the chemist, and her phantom slides across my inner eye. There she is again in her last years, so pretty and frail, attentively dressed – 'this cardigan goes with this blouse', 'only these pants and shoes', 'not these earrings, those earrings' – walking painfully with a stick, eyes bright as we visit each shop, rejecting fruit, food, books, flowers and clothing as 'not just exactly right'. It was not permitted to buy lamb chops from any butcher, only from one who knew how she liked them. Eve had made decisions about everything to do with the way she lived, and they had to be obeyed. Her will, her sparkling cynicism and her clear sight of things drove this small old woman to consider having tattoos to cover the flesh that had shrunk to almost nothing and bruised with dismaying ease on her legs, hands and arms. She thought that she should have her nose 'done' and her neck 'lifted'. She went to her hairdresser every week, and in the last weeks Mitch came to her. On the day of her death, I had brushed her hair away from her face, the way she liked. I checked her hair again when she was in her coffin, lying wrapped in the cream raw silk she had specified: 'cream, not white'. It was her spine, her insistence on perfection, that took her away from the desert town, the alcoholic father, the damaged, unhappy mother, and the beautiful, promiscuous sister, and brought her round the world to inhabit her own place with utter certainty. Still, she did not agree with the way she looked. 'It should have been different.' A year after her death, I found a photograph she had sent me. Written on the back was, *Here is the photograph of me you asked for.* When I turned it over, the only thing visible was the back of her head. She had the last laugh.

2001

It is a Monday fierce with sun, clouds spilt in the sky like white blossom, mountaintops laced with shadow patterns as we drive up the Great Western Highway. I remember this side of the road where yellow daisies used to grow beside the railway line – they still do. The bell-bird calls chime ringed tones at what we had nicknamed 'Bellbird Corner'. My mother rises in front of me as a young woman, driving home up the Blue Mountains to the farm. This is where she always stopped for a bag of fresh oranges. At Leura she would shop for camellias with Mr Sorenson, whom she held in high esteem, rare for her. She was thorough in a way I will never be thorough, always knowing how many blackberries to a pail, which bushes were good to pick from, how much sugar for jam, how long on the heat, when it was ready, exactly how long to boil the jars before the hot jam was ladled in, even when making it over a picnic fire.

Walking on the back farm one winter afternoon, a poisonous black snake suddenly coiled up her leg, and she kicked it away. In the same manner many years later, dancing with Secretary of State George Shultz at a ball in Washington, she kicked away her half-slip when its elastic gave way and twisted down her legs. She kept dancing.

'Oh, look at me, I'm dancing!'

*   *   *   *

Her mother, who had so little money, eked out family dinners with bread-and-butter pudding. When Ollie sang, 'Brown eyes, pickle pies / blue eyes, beauty', Eve would say to me, 'Don't worry, your sister has the looks, but you have personality.' I was appalled at what she had decided would be my fate and tried to perfect in my imagination a method to use if I happened to fall off a cliff. It involved turning somersaults in the air, springing up from the bottom of the precipice as if from a vaulting horse. Later, I decided I might become a scientist and tried out my new chemistry set in the living room, but was so obsessed with making blue from cobalt siccative that my only successful experiment was a giant blue stain that blotted the white carpet.

I remember this swoop of road up past Katoomba. How many times did I drive here with her? My chest constricts. This is where we always looked for the white memorial cross on the cliff where a climber had fallen to his death, somebody's son. Now I have a son who climbs. Once, driving down Victoria Pass, the brakes on our car failed and my father, a young handsome man, ran the car up a roadside cut to safety.

The brush beside the road seems not to have grown taller in all these intervening years. It feels as if the flora and fauna should have morphed into something different, just as I have. We pass Medlow Bath then the Mount Victoria Hotel, which looks out over the breathing blue bush, the escarpments and valleys. This is where I refused to spend my wedding night, aged twenty, hoping to reach Eve by phone when we got to Sydney to ask if I could come back home, now that I had gone through the ceremony and the reception, worn the dress, cut the cake. I hadn't wanted any of it but didn't know how to say this to the woman I had so consistently defied. 'She cannot come. She is outside looking at the stars,' my brother-in-law insisted when he answered the phone, and I found I had to be married after all.

*   *   *   *

Memories of my mother's last day suddenly sandbag me, of death encroaching her frail body. A blood vessel broke in her left eye, where years before the retina had detached. Slowly her eyeballs rolled up in their sockets and her mouth sagged open. Her nose had thinned to the bone. She would have liked the way it looked at last.

Her skin was delicately crumpled over her tiny complete bones, her mysterious skeleton. She was a sturdy woman once, too plump for her own liking. In my bedside drawer I keep, unwashed, the handkerchief I held dampened to her hot forehead on the last day of her life – in the same way that as a ten-year-old at boarding school I kept her handkerchief soaked in her Blue Grass perfume, as if I could inhale her.

Blackheath, and Perry's Lookdown – it is a long time since I was on this highway to Oberon and the farm. The European trees Eve loved are turning gold – cherries, maples, elms – European trees that are no longer popular, and I am ambushed by birdsong, watch magpies throw up their heads vertically, bills slightly parted, and want to put my finger on their throats to feel the warble pulsing there. Eve loved them, and it seems as if she is calling to me from their slender black-and-white feathered bodies.

Victoria Pass comes, and the steep descent where the brakes had failed my father. Eve had been angry, probably believing that she would have done better. There is now a sign alerting drivers: *Safety Ramp Ahead*. Below, the broad valley spills out like the Arthur Streeton painting *Still Glides the Stream and Shall Forever Glide*. There was once a teashop in this valley, where we would stop for scones with jam and cream. Next comes the little town of Hartley, with its apple trees, and finally the turn-off to Oberon.

I get out of the car and smell the fragrant bush, the sweetness of waiting raindrops. 'I am not ready,' I say, panicked, to Yale, who is driving, and instead we turn onto the road to Bathurst. Hammerhead clouds build above us, backlit with gold.

We are to stay in a tiny cottage in Hill End, and that night we hear the heavy breathing of cattle that, free to roam the town, are curled up beside the weathered fence. Inside are slanted ceilings, an old iron bed, sway-backed chairs with broken spines, low shaky lamps. Outside, the sky is sheared with gold as the sunset runs an aureate reef overhead, echoing the gold that once lay in the ground. This is my grandfather's sunset, and I have not seen one like it since I watched the movies he took in the early 1950s of endless sunsets over Broken Hill, the sky racked up with orange and gold.

In the morning, two scarlet parrots land on the roof of the studio in Hill End and drink from the gutters on the tin roof. There are fig trees in the garden, but something has eaten them: parrots, magpies or my mother? It was her favourite hiding place and I have not forgotten. 'I could hide in the fig tree, eat figs and pick grapes from the grapevine,' she said. I see her secretive child's face peering from under the leaves. Playing the scales. C-D-E-F-G-A-B-C. Reverse.

Beside the ruts and dust of the road, a few tiny bluebells grow, with piercing sky-blue petals and white stars in their centre. I used to pick them for Eve and their stems bled white sap onto my fingers. They are the last thought my mother gave to me without uttering a word, as I sat beside her bed on the final morning of her life, watching the deep unconsciousness of her terminal sleep. I thought I would try to take her on the trip we had promised her. Eve had wanted to fly one last time over the desert to see its flowers in bloom. She had been recording the rainfall for me and knew exactly how brilliant the flowers of her childhood would be. In my imagination we were there, high up over the earth scarlet with Sturt's peas when, with a brisk snap, five eastern mountain bluebells appeared in my head. Eve put them there, five hypnotic blue flowers. It was just what she would have done – chosen something completely at odds with my plan. I swear I heard her laughing deep in her bone dreams, though no sound came.

She had laughed from that other side when we came to the cottage at Hill End. It was the kind of cottage she had spent her life avoiding. She laughed and laughed. The kind of laugh that let you know she thought you a fool. Not the kind of fool she would be, with a mink coat, a Piaget watch and a husband who had been knighted. There were fig trees, parrots, and an old quince tree so tall we could not reach the fruit. A magpie sat on the fence, and Eve's mocking laughter stayed with me. In Australia the year before she died, I was walking barefoot up a bush track on the far side of Pittwater when I stopped to paint an angophora. As I dabbed at my small palette of watercolours, I felt something nudge my toes. It was an echidna, rolling its long spines against my foot. I must have obstructed its search for ants, or maybe it was just being friendly. 'See, you still belong,' Eve had said. 'You are still Australian. It is still your country.'

*   *   *   *

I stand at the garden gate of the little cottage in Hill End, say goodbye to my husband and slide backward in time. Did my grandmother do this, careful Olive Harradine, the youngest of seven, the English teacher from Maitland? Did she wait in a small garden with figs and quinces, washing pegged out to dry, plotting to buy a piano and change my mother's life? Jean would marry and sleep her way free of the small desert town, but not Eve. She would leave on wings of talent. 'Hope is the thing with feathers,' wrote Emily Dickinson. Were there enough to fly?

*　　　*　　　*　　　*

When I was seven, my mother took me to stay with Ollie, who then lived in a small apartment on the ground floor of a house in Sydney. Pressed for something to amuse a country child accustomed to running free, she accompanied me to a tennis match. When I needed to pee, she pointed to the dunny, a wooden shed with a toilet inside with a varnished wooden seat. 'Did you sit on the seat?' she demanded when I returned. 'Yes,' I replied, and she grabbed my hand, hurried me back to her apartment, pulled down my underpants, bent me over the white enamel tub and scrubbed my bottom almost raw with soap and a nail brush. Eve would have approved. She never sat on the seat.

At Hill End, when I go to the dunny at the end of the garden, I check the walls, the ceiling and the cracked cement floor for spiders before I sit. 'Don't sit on the seat!'

*　　　*　　　*　　　*

I am back in Balmoral now after the time in Hill End. 'I am so glad you were there,' my father says. 'It's the high country, and that's the country you grew up in, around Oberon, at 4000 feet. You were born in Broken Hill, but you grew up in the high country. I am glad you were there.'

The azure sky is fierce. The sun forces black light behind every rock, shrub and tree. A swimmer's arms hook like gull wings making dark cuts in the flux of silver sea. A white arc of sand is washed with translucent green. A slither of brackish charcoal luffs just below the surface, a remnant of the days when steamers discharged at sea just outside the Heads. The water slips like jelly over rocks. Gulls and cormorants rest on a curve of net that still encloses a half arc of beach, erected when sharks were said to take swimmers. The rest of the net is gone now, swimmers unafraid. Tree ferns spread out like green lace umbrellas, uncoiling their croziers to test the air, which is so quiet and calm it seems to be waiting patiently to be stroked, like a pet cat.

Light pierces everything here – even the cockatoo on the railing appears translucent, its lemony crest gilded with sun. Huge ships nudged by tugs make their way quickly out of the Heads, turning their vast bulk more swiftly than the eye can reckon. Little boats trace scarred wakes, burred silver pathways in the sea. In the late afternoon, small white yachts flutter and tip on the blue-green swells like butterflies on a leaf. On the wind comes the sound of sailors yelling, 'Come about!'

Late in the day, clouds rack up on each other in billowing pink-and-gold towers that slide over a grey underskirt. The whole span of water soaks up rose, and rapidly turns lilac as the light extinguishes. Then night rides the black water with a rough echo of yellow ripples. Roosting birds reach a crescendo of squeaks and squawks, fluttering and fluting, which mute abruptly with the loss of light. Big bogong moths swirl round indoor lights, beating their wings frantically above doorways and bed lamps, eyes reflecting a reddish gleam. This is an island. I look out and see the land flatten into sandstone cliffs. Standing on the balcony at night, I watch as the sky settles into pink striped clouds, cockatoos, kookaburras, currawongs and magpies streaking to roost, as I have watched them do for the last thirty-five years whenever I return to this balcony. A small luff of waves breaks on the beach while pelicans float aimlessly. The sky darkens and I see the light on North Head, then Middle Head and, across it, South Head's brighter lights and the vast, empty Pacific. A few little green and red lights bob, small boats night-fishing. The stars align themselves and take up their silent positions as if in a ballet class, the Southern Cross or Crux, shaped like one.

The small ferry hurries to Manly, lights a dizzy smear on the water. A trace of smoke laces the air, Australia's signature smell of burning. The dark Heads outline themselves against a wash of silver, settling in for sleep, the billowy lights, the melaleucas, the gums and Christmas bush, the angophoras sway and turn their leaves sideways, whistling in the dark. A last car turns quickly down the street towards the quiet bay. Awaba Street is solitary as it empties into the ocean, upending into blue. Nothing stirs. There is no moon. Tomorrow the magpies will thread the air too early with artful cadence, then sleep will continue until the kookaburras cough and snigger like rheumy gents with wormy lungs after a night of whisky and cigarettes: 'Hahahahahahehehehhehohohohokoffkaff!'

The day bursts over the horizon in a trumpet blast of colour, taking no prisoners, air fragrant with bruised eucalypt. Clouds blur over North Head like smeared chalk. In the distance, vast tropical clouds tower into white hammerheads, and lightning strikes the earth in violet zippers from clouds as moody as adolescents. There is coffee downstairs, the splatter of someone showering, toast burning, birds waiting to be fed. Over and over this happens, and I am not here. I know it but am not known, leaving renders you invisible, dying fixes you in place.

2002

Two years after Eve died, I return and dig up her ashes, which my father had planted under a white rose bush in the apartment garden. She had been very clear her ashes were to go in the ocean. Her instructions were to wrap her in a length of cream raw silk, nothing more, her hair done properly, no makeup, and cremated. I dig up the sickly white rose, then dig deeper to be certain I have gathered all her ashes mixed with earth, put them in a bag filled with frangipani from the tree on the corner, and replant the rose. I ride the ferry, the *Sirius*, from Neutral Bay to Circular Quay on Saturday, 7 December 2002. At 11.30 a.m. at mid-harbour, off the right bow of the ferry, facing the Conservatorium of Music and the Botanical Gardens, just past Government House, I pour Eve's ashes into the sea. She will wash up on the shores of music and back again to Government House, where she attended so many receptions as Lady Cotton, little Bebe, Cousin Eve, Eve Macdougall from William Street in Broken Hill. The frangipani floats in the churning wake of the ferry.

When I see the Harbour Bridge from the ferry, I remember her holding onto the last shreds of her life to watch the century turn, to see *ETERNITY* spelt out in fireworks, as if it were a private message for her. I see Luna

Park's inane smiling face, where she took us as children to slither screaming down the long wooden slides. Returning from the ferry, I stop to see Mitch, who did her hair in hospital three days before she died. He tells me, 'I loved that woman. Now, don't get me wrong, when I first met her, I thought, I don't know if this will work. But by the end she was the woman with whom I had the best relationship in my life.'

It is a bright, windy day, with a north-west wind. 'May your spirit live, may you spend millions of years, you who love Thebes, sitting with your face to the north wind, your eyes beholding happiness,' I say. When we buried my little white-faced dog six months after Eve died, we wrote the same thing on his coffin, an inscription on a lotus 'Wishing Cup' discovered in the entrance to Tutankhamen's tomb. I said the same thing over my husband's ashes when he died suddenly fourteen years later, after a forty-year love affair. Yale, the only man I ever loved.

*   *   *   *

I used to wonder what I brought to the family other than obstinacy. But looking back, I remembered that I could make them laugh, entertain them with long stories of

worlds I built in my imagination. After her death, I found
a letter Eve wrote to me, dated 25 June 1972.

*Your letter reached us in Melbourne eventually,
and I can't tell you how much it has meant to
us. I don't know why we Anglo Saxons find it
hard to give expression to our feelings – early
training or perhaps the result of hurts when
one has let one's feelings go. Therefore, when
it does happen, I think it has much more depth
and impact. I have composed many beautiful
letters standing under the shower or travelling in
the car – you know the kind of wonderful letters
mothers should write. But now I am actually
writing my fluency and expression have left me.
Why don't you live next door? Then I could have
come over and shed a few sentimental tears with
you and told you how I feel. But if you lived next
door maybe you'd never have said those things.
You'd have known me too well and wouldn't have
liked me enough to say them.*

*As for me, giving to you was always easy.
You were a really delightful little girl, healthy,
imaginative and happy – naughty though. You
were such a joy to be with. When you became*

unhappy in your later teens, it hit me with an awful thud. It always annoyed me that Gannie [Ollie] could not see that she favoured Anne above you two – she would get very hurt if I said so. Please tell me if I do it because I don't feel it.

*   *   *   *

Sitting at Neutral Bay on the tiny terrace of Eve's favourite cafe, overlooking the water, I drink coffee. She loved coffee so much that, even pregnant with me, she drank twelve cups a day. She had a hand-cranked coffee grinder mounted on the wall. The beans were poured into the metal top, ground by turning the handle to achieve a fine powder, fresh every time, the way she liked it. I never told my father I moved her ashes, but my sister and her girls were glad. The very last secret Eve heard before she died was my sister whispering that my niece Catriona was pregnant with a baby girl, to be named for her, Sophie Eve. My mother smiled, the miracle of birth present just as she was dying.

From the ferry, I go back to the apartment and, while my father is in the kitchen, touch Eve's things to say goodbye, two years since she died. He doesn't notice what I am doing, but as soon as I am done, he hands me an invitation to his wedding and, breathless, I feel as if I have just got Eve out in time. 'Your mother would be pleased,' people say to me, meaning well. Get a grip, I think, she would be furious. He belonged to Eve.

VIII

'You have a pain face,' Eve said to me, as I sat beside her bed in intensive care yet again. I had been waiting with my father and sister for six anxious weeks as she hovered between life and death after a second heart bypass. Now her consciousness had returned, but not the curb on her tongue. It was not what I wanted to hear, but I knew it was true.

Thirty years after Tony spun out of the sky, pain knocked me from my bike to sit beside the road, panting. Clumps of unravelled fern were laced with poison ivy; the air was heavy with pollen and the perfume of wild briar. My husband found me later and took me home and laid me down stuffed with painkillers.

Like the blue wave that caught Tony, the pain would ebb, gauzy and insubstantial, only to swamp back so fiercely it drowned my power of thought. Doctors claimed that I was the problem: 'You paint the wrong way. You have the wrong priorities. You are from New York. You must. You must not. Don't do this. Do that. Relax.' But as the tide of symptoms washed around me unattended, my brain was sucked out of reach in the undertow.

I pried a tick from its blood lock on my ankle to show the doctors. 'No, you tested negative,' they responded. And my fuzzy brain had forgotten the other squashed and bloody ticks. My body slowly twisted into semi-immobility and soon I was in a wheelchair, unable to walk or stand. Late Lyme disease – caused by bacteria transmitted by the bite of a tick – had hit my spine and brain. But no doctor seemed to believe a tick could do this. No painkillers reached me. I was my own nightmare, a writhing creature from one of Hieronymus Bosch's fantastical imagery. Words came out backwards. Meaning eluded me. I forgot my own name. Tadpoles swam in my brain, spirochaetes that were eating up my memory and ability to survive. I spent half a year in a wheelchair, unable to walk or stand, and three years in bed, struggling to find myself again. Eve wanted to come and help but Yale, knowing her fragility, said no, he would do it. And he did. Taught me to walk again. When I sat beside her bed at last, Eve said coolly, 'I didn't think your brain would recover.' But she had sent me a crossword puzzle every day until it did.

*   *   *   *

Now, I slowly walk where Tony once walked, tracing
the arc of jetty that encloses an old swimming pool in
the ocean at Balmoral. The white-topped pylons are
encrusted with weed and oysters. Did Tony swim here,
listening to the clink of boats alongside, the suck and
swallow of the sea, watching shivers of small fish ruffle
the water into goosebumps? The noon sun crochets rip-
pled pink-and-green reflections on white boat hulls. An
aftershock of apricot sun on the sea bounces back into
the sky, air to water, so that they marry and cannot be
parted. The tiny information of the day hides itself in
hibiscus, jasmine, sugar ants, spider webs, the oozy rot-
ten whiffs of gas in the streets, in etiolated palms swaying
clipped pineapple heads, green-and-yellow ferries passing by. There is a sunspot on the sea, a line of silver drawn
straight and sparkling on the horizon. The edge of the
land is pale gold, the sea translucent green as if lit by a
lamp at the continent's eroding edge. House lights bloom
and the silent house ticks.

*   *   *   *

When my sister phoned, it was raining. She had just come
back from the Vietnam War memorial in Mittagong.
My father had bought a cherry tree for Tony, and he
planted it with my mother. I thought of them, both in

their eighties, shovelling earth for the nephew loved so long ago. Tony's mother, Pauline – my father's oldest sister – came from Queensland with John, now the eldest of her children. He wore his military uniform and medals, and when a woman asked why he wore medals on the right shoulder as well as the left, he said, 'I am wearing my brother's medals.' I wept when I heard this, and my sister – far away under her own rainy skies – wept too. 'I found out how it happened,' she said. 'He was returning to Saigon from a rescue mission when his helicopter hit some wires and went down in flames.' This wasn't the way I had pictured it. Flames, yes, were there flames? Did it matter? Dead is dead. Except, for me, Tony never is.

*   *   *   *

The sea has blue lips. Fishing boats swing in its harbour, taking their cue from the wind. Sunlight flashes from windscreens across the water. Little fish dizzy the shallows, where a small riff of black weed washes. Propped on one red leg, gulls hunker down, heads tucked back over their shoulders. A quick scuff of wind ruffles the water. Square-nosed and rimmed with rust, fishing boats tethered inside the breakwater buck against tyres lashed to the dock. Beyond lies the sea, a great gape of blue, yawning vacantly, and hiccups of froth fret the tops of the waves. There are huge crumbs of rock at the bottom of the sandstone cliffs, and straggling eucalypt, bunched and ragged, cling there. A man in sandals walks along the beach, carrying a pair of children's shoes in one hand. Parrots squeak.

Driving north along Australia's endless coast of empty golden beaches, air fizzing with salt spray, we smell the spoor print of each town – fish frying with chips. We have come from my brother's house in Canberra, where we ate figs from his trees and walked with him every night with his dog along the street overarched with tall American elms. Elm Street was once one of the most common street names in America, after Main Street. 'Just like America twenty years ago, fifty years ago, or a hundred years ago,' people like to say of Australia. It is nothing like America. Never suffered from its terminal innocence, blighted, and dying now, as the elms and chestnuts died.

*   *   *   *

A long silver wave rolls over me and breaks my heart, as I wake and find again you are not here. For the rest of my life, you will not be here. Magpies carol in Australia's vast loneliness, an empty day under a vacant sky. Below is the faint sound of waves licking the sea's lips on a wide white curve of sand; the gum trees are lacy and forgiving. Lantanas cast violet light, spilling a halo of colour onto the ground. It is always Eve's ghost I see in that luminous shower.

I will walk on the beach rocks and feel the continent hum under my bare feet. I will float on green waves and spill something of myself into the day, my presence a tiny inkblot on this vast land, stained with the murders of its traditional custodians, a land stolen by those of my kind who came here and fell in love. I will be sieved with warm sand, absorb the blatant bird call that owns the air. Then I will leave again, attempting to evade the land and people that still hold me prisoner, shake off its fierce undertow. I try to shield myself as the nictitating blue inner eyelid of a kookaburra flicks and swiftly shuts out the world. I resist the invisible feelers that creep like tiny heat-seeking missiles to cut to my core. I cannot afford to feel. Age has taught me that. I leave again.

No one's story can explain the past.

No one story.

ACKNOWLEDGEMENTS

To my son, Tim Cotton, his wife, Anne Laure Py, their two wonderful daughters, my granddaughters Juliette and Charlotte Cotton, for the love and bliss they bring to my life.

My beloved brother and sister, Robert Cotton and Anne Ferguson.

Bob and Eve Cotton, whose amazing path in life made this possible.

Thanks go to my extended family of aunts, uncles, cousins, nieces and nephew. Particular thanks go to Gini Cotton, Catriona Andrews and the Py family.

My deepest gratitude to the brilliant, erudite writer and my friend Sebastian Smee; Lowery Stokes Sims, deservedly famous curator, scholar and friend for thirty years; Caro Llewelyn, to whom I can spill my heart; and Diana Simmonds, my dazzling soul sister.

Thanks to Cynthia Beglin, the gifted writer and friend who is my first reader, Anna Kneeland for unfailing encouragement, Marguerite d'Aprile Quigley, Janet Slater, Ally Spurling, Kathryn Lee and Mary Coyle, Juliet Rogers, Stewart Waltzer, Richard Lightfoot, Fritz Jellinghaus, Lyn and Terry Fern and Sprague Theobald, who set such a sterling example of courage in his *The Other Side of the Ice*.

Deep gratitude also to Denise and Paul Mineau, who make my life and art possible in so many ways.

Not least, but truly foremost in this list, are Sophy Williams and Rebecca Bauert of Black Inc. Books. Thank you for taking this chance on me. Beck, you are an incredible editor and know how to guide when a writer's foot stumbles, to clearly see structure and be the metronome that sets the book's true rhythm.

I am grateful for Charles Green's Tate Paper 'Notes on the Centre', about that formative 1967 exhibition 'Two Decades of American Painting in Australia', mentioned on page 97. See www.tate.org.uk/research/tate-papers/32/two-decades-american-painting

I would like to thank the collectors of my art, the museums, curators, directors and galleries who have made my journey possible: the Metropolitan Museum of Art, the National Gallery of Australia, the Phillips Collection, the Florence Griswold Museum, the Lyman Allyn Museum, Hazelhurst Regional Gallery, Bathurst Regional Art Gallery, and the Bundanon and Hill End artist residencies. Particular thanks to Sam Quigley, visionary director of the Lyman Allyn Museum.

And to Yale Kneeland, art lover, adventurer, race car driver, cowboy and art conservator.

And finally, gratitude for the Australian continent, which holds my heart.

Eve

Robert Cotton, Leslie Cotton and R.C. Cotton

Eve and Bob on their wedding day, next to Tony's mother,
Pauline, and Monty Cotton

Jean, Anne and Ollie Macdougall (Harradine)

Monty Cotton

Bob in the air force

Judy and Eve

Rob

Wading in the Duckmaloi

Anne and Judy at boarding school

Rob, Tony and Squeak with Cheeky the Ram

Rob and Judy at Palm Beach

Bob announces his political campaign against
Prime Minister Ben Chifley

Judy, Rob and Anne, Oberon Farm, Long Paddock

Eve and Bob with her prize Hampshire Downs

Bob Cotton

Tim

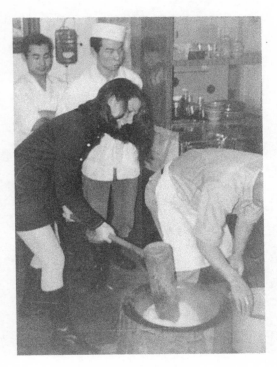

Judy in Tokyo

Sir Robert and Lady Cotton at Buckingham Palace

Judy, Eve and Anne

Bob and Judy, Barrenjoey Head

Painting Nature Morte *in studio*

Judy

9 781760 643